BIBLICAL COUNSELING REVIEWS

of

Dr. Jay Adams
Dr. David Powlison
Dr. Heath Lambert
Dr. John Street
Dr. Jim Newheiser
Dr. Paul Tripp
Pastor Randy Patten

Martin & Deidre Bobgan

Scripture quotations are taken from the Authorized King James Version of the Bible, except as otherwise indicated.

This book includes modified compilations of former writings by Martin and Deidre Bobgan: *Christ-Centered Ministry versus Problem-Centered Counseling*; *Person to Person Ministry*; *"Counseling the Hard Cases": A Critical Review*; *Stop Counseling! Start Ministering!* and articles from *PsychoHeresy Awareness Letter*.

Biblical Counseling Reviews

Published by EastGate Publishers
4137 Primavera Road
Santa Barbara, CA 93110

Library of Congress Control Number 2018910704
ISBN 978-0941717-27-4

Printed in the United States of America

Let the words of my mouth, and the meditation of my heart, be acceptable in thy sight, O Lord, my strength and my redeemer.

Psalm 19:14

For more information on

Martin and Deidre Bobgan's

writings see

PsychoHeresy Awareness Ministries

at

www.pamweb.org/mainpage.html

Table of Contents

1

Sin-Saturated Biblical Counseling

Biblical Counseling Reviews of Dr. Jay Adams, Dr. David Powlison, Dr. Heath Lambert, Dr. John Street, Dr. Jim Newheiser, Dr. Paul Tripp, and Pastor Randy Patten reveals that the best examples of biblical counseling done by some of the foremost leaders of the biblical counseling movement (BCM) have grave biblical errors. **We have repeatedly said that the undoing of the biblical counseling movement does not primarily come from their teachings, but from their practices and presentations of actual counseling when examined with the Bible**. This book is an exposé of what seven of the recognized leaders and teachers of biblical counseling actually do in counseling and why believers should shun their counseling conversations. In presenting the practices and presentations of those in the BCM, we use the terms "counseling," "counselor," and "counselee," because that is their terminology. We discuss the errors of using such terms in Appendices A and B; we offer replacements for these words in Appendix C; and **in Appendix D we provide Scriptures that are rarely,**

if ever, used by biblical counselors, but are regularly violated during counseling conversations. The irony is that these are the very Bible verses that are violated during biblical counseling thereby enabling sinful conversations. Therefore we suggest reading the verses in Appendix D before reading the reviews of the seven biblical counselors.

It is strange that there is such a reluctance to name names of those in the biblical counseling movement who are involved in unbiblical practices when Dr. Jay Adams, who fathered the modern-day, newly arrived movement, wrote the following in his endorsement for our book *PsychoHeresy: The Psychological Seduction of Christianity*, defending us for doing so:

> Some people will say the Bobgans are hitting too hard—naming names and all that—but I don't think so. Whenever someone writes for the Christian public he sets forth his views to the scrutiny of others, but if others think what he says is dangerous to the church they, like Paul (who named names too), have an obligation to say so.[1]

Adams has also said elsewhere:

> Any Christian who sets himself up as a teacher in the church of Christ and publicly teaches anything thereby opens himself up for criticism by others (cf. James 3:1). If they think what he is teaching is harmful to the church, they have an obligation to point it out just as widely as it was taught. Such public warning or debate on a topic should not be considered a personal attack at all.... What a critic of a public teaching does in pointing out his disagreement with that teaching

> has nothing to do with personal affronts or lack of reconciliation; he is simply disagreeing at the same public level as that on which the teaching was given in the first place.[2]

In 1985 Moody Press published our book titled *How to Counsel from Scripture*.[3] At that time we were an active part of the biblical counseling movement. However, **after discovering what those in the biblical counseling movement were actually doing during their counseling, we departed from the movement.** That was many years ago! At the time we asked Moody Press to put the book out of print, because we could no longer recommend it in the various ways it supported the BCM. As we looked more deeply into the movement we could see that it incorporated the same kinds of sin-saturated conversations as the psychological counseling movement. To explain our concerns and the reasons for departing from the BCM, we wrote *Against "Biblical Counseling": For the Bible*.[4]

Since then we have extensively written material revealing that the literal counseling conducted by the leaders of the BCM fails when examined biblically. The chapters in this book expose the veiled truth that the leaders of the three generations of biblical counselors are in biblical error as they have imbibed from the polluted streams of psychological counseling in their integration, eclecticism, and pragmatism.

There is some excellent biblical material in the various biblical counseling manuals, books, and certificate and degree programs. However, we repeat: the major undoing of the biblical counseling movement is found in their literal counseling and case studies. It is their Achilles heel! **The good biblical material is undone by their live counseling, which reveals what they actually do.** However, many of the cases they describe in their writings lack the real conversations and dialogues that typically go on in biblical counseling. There are thousands of biblical counseling books, videos, and audios, but **not many have literal cases with detailed dialogue. The best way to recognize the unbiblical nature of biblical counseling is to read or hear and evaluate available literal, live (not simply playacted) counseling by using biblical standards. There one can see and hear how the counseling problems are discussed and what sinful conversations are actually involved.** They are similar to psychological counseling in that they are heavily problem-centered in the most unbiblical ways and often involve sinful speaking.

In this book we use material from a number of our past books and articles, which reveal that biblical counseling as constructed and conducted is sinful to the core. **Because much of this book was taken and modified from a variety of our past writings, there is some repetition of expressions and comments from one critical review to another.**

In the following chapters we present the biblical counseling of Dr. Jay Adams, the father of the modern-day biblical counseling movement, and six other internationally recognized leaders of the BCM. They are Dr. David Powlison, Dr. Heath Lambert, Dr. John Street, Dr. Jim Newheiser, Dr. Paul Tripp, and Pastor Randy Patten. Having originated and developed what he called "nouthetic counseling," Adams was the first generation of the Johnny-come-lately biblical counseling movement. The second generation of the BCM is the "idols of the heart" nouthetic variation fathered by Powlison. The third generation of nouthetic counseling is proposed in Lambert's book *The Biblical Counseling Movement After Adams*. Lambert himself appears to be the leader of the third generation of nouthetic counseling and its variations with his "Grand Unifying Theory."[5] Street, Newheiser, Tripp, and Patten are also significant, world-wide recognized leaders of the BCM.

As Adams and the other six counselors engage in sinful conversations, they are reflecting the sinful conversations of psychotherapy. Therefore they reveal that they are all integrationists in that they add the sinful conversational ways of psychotherapy to the Bible. The counseling conversations done by these seven counselors are examples of the way biblical counseling is practiced by many throughout the church who are also emulating conversational aspects of psychological counseling. An added advantage of reading the seven biblical counseling reviews is that one will also be able to understand that the same unbibical faults exist in psychotherapeutic conversations.

In this book we critically review what these leaders of the BCM actually do in their counseling to demonstrate that **what they do is definitely and decisively NOT entirely biblical**! The chapter on Adams, who founded the movement, and the chapters on other recognized leaders who followed him will show how unbiblical they truly are as they actually counsel individuals. While reading about the counseling in the following chapters, note how specific biblical prescriptions and restrictions are violated against parents, spouses, and others.

Problem-Centered Counseling

Because of the problem-centered conversations of both psychological and biblical counseling, the counselor will ask numerous questions to find out what the problems are and then ask further probing questions for clarification and detail. **Considering that counselors direct the counseling conversations through their questions, they are truly the instigators and enablers of the resulting sinful communication.** That does not excuse the participating counselees who are ready and eager to speak their minds (generally filled with sinful thoughts when one considers what is said). **Notice how the counselors in the following chapters precipitate the sinful expressions of Jeremiah 17:9 as they probe for problems, dig for details, and thereby conduct counselees into sinning with their tongues in violation of many biblical prescriptions, proscriptions, admonitions, expectations, and warnings.**

> The heart is deceitful above all things, and desperately wicked: who can know it? I the LORD search the heart, I try the reins, even to give every man according to his ways, and according to the fruit of his doings. (Jer. 17:9-10.)

Jeremiah 17:9 hearts contaminate problem-centered counseling as counselees are given free rein to talk about the sins of others not present, including unsubstantiated talebearing and hearsay, without being restricted, contradicted, or investigated. Because counseling is considered confidential, counselees naturally skew their stories, which are generally filled with much unsubstantiated self-bias, gossip, and hearsay. In addition, the counselor's flesh may also be activated in a number of ways, particularly in the pride of being the wise one to counsel the needy one in the one-up/one-down counseling environment.[6] Not only can counselors be self-deceived as far as their own importance in the lives of fellow believers, but **these seven counselors are sinning dreadfully by permitting and enabling others to sin through their speaking**. These counselors not only precipitate sinful communication through questions that elicit evil speaking; but they also provide a private place and an ear to hear corrupt conversations as they continue to pry and probe. Perhaps they would say that the end justifies the means, but when does God ask us to sin that grace may abound (Rom. 6:1)? As you read the following chapters, take note of the talebearing and hearsay that is heard, enabled, and even encouraged by the biblical counselors.

Words are powerful and revealing. James describes the power of words in the human tongue:

> If any man offend not in word, the same is a perfect man, and able also to bridle the whole body.... And the tongue is a fire, a world of iniquity: so is the tongue among our members, that it defileth the whole body, and setteth on fire the course of nature; and it is set on fire of hell.... But the tongue can no man tame; it is an unruly evil, full of deadly poison. (James 3:2b, 6, 8.)

Notice the devastating nature of some of the sinful statements made by counselors and counselees in the following chapters and compare the conversations with James 3.

Words can carry great destructive power and they also reveal the person's spiritual condition. A few unkind words can ignite a battle between persons, groups, and nations. Words can be poison to the soul, both of the speaker and hearer. The fire kindled by the tongue can start with a spark of talebearing, which can lead to misunderstanding, ill feelings, acrimony, animosity, bitterness, and the destroying of other people's privacy to the point of growing into a wildfire. However, **Bible verses that warn about the danger of the tongue were never used by the seven counselors to curb a counselee's communication during these counseling sessions. Neither did these seven counselors take the biblical responsibility to protect their counselees from violating biblical restraints on the tongue.**

How important is our conversation with one another? The Bible has much to say about how individuals are to communicate with each other. Jesus Himself taught about the serious significance of words:

> But I say unto you, that every idle word that men shall speak, they shall give account thereof in the day of judgment. For by thy words thou shalt be justified, and by thy words thou shalt be condemned. (Matt. 12:35-37.)

In reference to Jesus's words to the Pharisees, Albert Barnes says that the term "idle word" "literally means a vain, thoughtless, useless word; a word that accomplishes no good. Here it means, evidently, 'wicked, injurious, false, malicious,' for such were the words which they had spoken."[7] Idle, careless words can easily tear down relationships. An idle, careless word demeaning a wife or complaining about a husband has the power to unravel a one-flesh relationship—one thread at a time by a few words at a time. Note the lack of restraint in the counseling cases in the following chapters.

When people describe their problems as being communication problems, they are talking about talk—conversation—both speaking and listening. We are living in a day of unrestrained talk, much motivated by hurt feelings, anger, frustration, self-protection, victim-mentality, and various sinful responses to circumstances and people. One book criticizes Americans as being *A Nation of Victims*[8] and another book documents *A Narcissism Epidemic*[9] running amok in the nation. How grievous to see how much of this is going on in much of the biblical counseling being practiced and promoted today, as can be seen in the following cases.

The sinful heart of Jeremiah 17:9 can erupt in all forms of corrupt communication that is sinful, depraved, evil, contaminating, harmful, obscene, or offensive and that would devalue another person. The Bible says: "Let no corrupt communication proceed out of your mouth, but that which is good to the use of edifying, that it may minister grace unto the hearers" (Eph. 4:29). **However, such corrupt communication is a crucial component in the counseling of the seven significant leaders of the biblical counseling movement.** Note the sin-saturated verbal violations of Ephesians 4:29 in the following chapters.

Counseling is full of sinful, self-biased conversations when the natural man speaks from a deceptive heart (Jeremiah 17:9). The counseling environment will free the counselee to justify self, put self's desires and so-called needs high on the priority list, and distort truth, directly or indirectly. People generally do not think of themselves as being part of the reason for their interpersonal problems. Many directly or indirectly deny their own penchant for sin and overlook actual sins they have committed. However, the Bible says, "If we say that we have no sin, we deceive ourselves, and the truth is not in us" (1 John 1:8).Therefore, there is much sinful self-deception in the counseling room, to the degree that the counselor will be hearing slanted tales. One has to wonder how counselors can really know what is truly going on with all the deception and self-deception on the part of both the counselees and the counselors. In fact, the more counselors dig for details, the more misinformation they will be receiving. Notice how the counselors in the following chapters dig for more and are thereby being deceived into thinking they are obtaining true and complete, uncontaminated information.

One of the verses that has become a standard at the beginning of many of the counseling cases, given as the reason for digging into the past and present personal lives, is Proverbs 18:13: "He that answereth a matter before he heareth it, it is folly and shame unto him." This verse sets the stage at the beginning of many of the counseling cases we have observed. However, it is falsely applied, as all counselors would have to hear from all the people their counselees talk about behind their backs. Counselees naturally describe their problems from a self-biased perspective and often see themselves as the injured ones. However, "He that is first in his own cause seemeth just; but his neighbour cometh and searcheth him" (Prov. 18:17). Counselors do not investigate whether or not a counselee's words about other people are accurate. That is why much counseling turns into kangaroo-court proceedings, where people (who have been talked about behind their backs) are condemned and convicted without a hearing and without witnesses to testify as to the truth. Of course the Bible is clear on this.

Shortly after the apostle Paul expressed his concern about "debates, envyings, wraths, strifes, backbitings, whisperings, swellings, tumults" (2 Cor 12:20), he declares: "In the mouth of two or three witnesses shall every word be established" (2 Cor. 13:1). Counselees often speak evil about others who are not present, including parents and spouses. As they do so, they will likely become further convinced of their own words, having had a ready ear in the counselor, who is taking everything seriously as in the following counseling cases.

As counselors in the following chapters ask for detailed descriptions of interpersonal problems, they are often eliciting one-sided, therefore biased, talebearing, which ends up being sinful, unsubstantiated gossip. The Bible clearly warns against such communication: "The words of a talebearer are as wounds, and they go down into the innermost parts of the belly" (Prov. 26:22). As counselors hear the tales, their thoughts about the person in the tale will influence them in relation to that person. This can be especially serious when tales are told about a spouse, parent, or other family members. Such sinful communication has torn apart families as counselors tend to believe what counselees say and as counselees often receive whatever sympathy or understanding is given as support. Not only will the listener of the tale receive contamination and the person about whom the tale is told get a bad rap, but the speaker (counselee) may also increase in bitterness towards that person. Talebearing can easily include slander, about which the Bible says: "A man that beareth false witness against his neighbour is a maul, and a sword, and a sharp arrow" (Prov. 25:18). Watch for the talebearing in the following chapters.

The seriousness of talebearing increases in relation to the blasphemy, which is evil speaking about humans as well as against God, about which the Bible warns in Colossians 3:8: "But now ye also put off all these; anger, wrath, malice, blasphemy, filthy communication out of your mouth." Notice how blasphemy or evil speaking is connected to anger, wrath, malice, and filthy communication, which can include all kinds of statements, from unkind remarks and descriptions of other people to what most consider to be "filthy." All of these expressions spew forth in the following cases as the seven counselors call for more details and as counselees are encouraged to tell all.

As you read the following cases, you will find expressions of sinful anger, as if such expressions are necessary or at least acceptable in counseling, in spite of the biblical warnings regarding anger. Yes, there are times to be angry, but it must be without sin: "Be ye angry, and sin not: let not the sun go down upon your wrath" (Eph. 4:26). Anger expressed in counseling is often sinful, because the person has either felt offended or is not getting wants satisfied. Therefore the Bible warns, "Be not hasty in thy spirit to be angry: for anger resteth in the bosom of fools" (Ecc. 7:9). In fact, rather than providing a platform for angry expressions, counselors should teach, "A wrathful man stirreth up strife: but he that is slow to anger appeaseth strife" (Prov. 15:18).

As one can see in the following chapters, all of these serious flaws of counseling reveal that the central problem of loving oneself more than God and others is allowed to flourish in counseling. The following counseling environments elicit many egregious forms of self-exonerating sinful speaking about others and self-justifying talk about self. Such sinful speaking would not happen if love for others were the foundation of the counseling conversations. However, we are living in those last days described in 2 Timothy 3:1-5:

> This know also, that in the last days perilous times shall come. For men shall be lovers of their own selves, covetous, boasters, proud, blasphemers, disobedient to parents, unthankful, unholy, without natural affection, trucebreakers, false accusers, incontinent, fierce, despisers of those that are good, traitors, heady, highminded, lovers of pleasures more than lovers of God. Having a form of godliness, but denying the power thereof: from such turn away.

Marriage Counseling

Sin-laden counseling, as done in the following chapters, is especially damaging to marriages with its open door to listing and describing the faults and sins of the spouse, parents, and others. Ephesians 5:22-33 regarding the marriage relationship is violated as questions open the door for the husband to criticize, demean, and complain about his wife and for the wife to criticize, dishonor, and complain about her husband. As couples are encouraged to tell all, there are too many opportunities for husbands and wives to damage their relationship through ill-spoken words to and about each other. One marriage counselor's mantra, shared by many, is:

> **Tell it, down to the last detail which you have confided to no man, and which nearly chokes you to bring out. Don't stop with this year, or the year before, but keep digging back into your life. It will be hard. It will hurt.**[10] (Bold added.)

Unfortunately in this kind of counseling much harm comes during the data gathering sessions. The marriage is supposed to be a picture of Christ and the church (Eph. 5: 31-32). However, as each spouse bites and devours the other through sinful, self-biased communication, a sorry picture is presented and generally accepted by the counselor for the time being, with the promise to help the couple out in future meetings. Notice how that happens in one or two of the following chapters as problems after problems are mentioned, with the primary "hope" being the counselor's commitment to counsel them for many weeks or months.

Another serious error in the biblical counseling in the following chapters is the one-up role of the counselor, which is particularly troublesome in marriage counseling. When counselors take the leadership role in the marriage relationship, they usurp the husband's role of headship (Eph. 5:23). Notice especially in Chapter 8 how Patten's authoritative command of "No Bible, no TV" demeans the husband in the wife's presence. Talking down to a husband in front of his wife could easily discourage her from honoring her husband (Eph. 5:33).

In their misguided attempts to help, several of the counselors in the following chapters pry into private matters that should be left alone, such as the marriage bed. In doing so they are encouraging counselees to sinfully reveal private matters. Because what is said in the counseling room is to be strictly confidential, counselees' tales often reveal secrets: "A talebearer revealeth secrets: but he that is of a faithful spirit concealeth the matter" (Prov. 11:13). Newheiser performs sex counseling in two of his cases that follow (Chapter 6) and he heads the organization that staged Lambert's egregious sex counseling with a porn addict and his wife described in Chapter 4. In Chapter 8 we show how Patten's directive "Describe" opens the door for the husband to sinfully complain about their sex life.

Along with the damaging biblical violations during marriage counseling are those that have to do with other family relationships, primarily parents. Ever since Freud put the blame for present-life struggles on the parents and primarily the mother, people have been blaming their parents both in and out of counseling. Parents have been not only criticized, but excoriated in the counseling environment, particularly when they are not there to defend themselves. Biblical counseling should be building up the family instead of tearing it down. All children are composites of both parents. Therefore, counseling that allows and even elicits talk that dishonors parents is destructive to the counselees themselves when they are given occasions to cast blame, criticize, and even castigate their parents. Dishonoring parents during counseling will more likely harm, rather than explain or fix marriages. The Bible places great importance on children, including adult children, honoring their parents: "Honour thy father and mother; (which is the first commandment with promise;) That it may be well with thee, and thou mayest live long on the earth" (Eph. 6:2-3). **Five of**

the following chapters involve counselees dishonoring their parents without any words of warning, as the counselors dig and delve.

Conclusion

Such sin-saturated conversations, as in the following chapters, did not originate from Scripture or from sound biblical teaching. They came from the sinful conversations of the psychological counseling movement as counselors followed the lead of Adams, who set the gold standard, which others followed. Instead of fully replacing the worldly, sinful, secular models and methods of psychological counseling, the leaders of the biblical counseling movement simply retrofitted the pattern of their conversations into their so-called biblical replacement. Then as many of the leaders of the biblical counseling movement recycled conversations from the polluted behavioristic, psychoanalytic, humanistic, and family systems streams of counseling psychology, they picked up the practices of sinful secular talk from these various psychotherapies. Reading the seven counselor reviews that follow should make it apparent that, **because of the many sinful conversations that occur in both psychological and biblical counseling, Christians should not be participants or practitioners in either one.**

2

Dr. Jay Adams

The Institute for Nouthetic Studies states that "Dr. Adams is the founder of the modern biblical counseling movement and is the author of the groundbreaking book *Competent to Counsel*. He is also the founder of the Institute for Nouthetic Studies (INS), the National Association of Nouthetic Counselors (NANC), and the Christian Counseling and Educational Foundation (CCEF)."[1] Adams has written over one hundred books, which have been translated into sixteen different languages.

In his book *Competent to Counsel*, Adams reveals that he worked one summer under Dr. O Hobart Mowrer, who was a research professor of psychology. Adams says:

> During the summer of 1965 we worked in two state mental institutions, one at Kankakee, Illinois, and the other at Galesburg, Illinois. In these two mental institutions, we conducted group therapy with Mowrer for seven hours a day. Along with five others, I flew with him, drove with him, ate with him five days a week. I learned much during that time, and while today I certainly would not classify myself as a member of Mow-

> rer's school, I feel that the summer program was **a turning point in my thinking.**[2] (Bold added.)

The turning point in Adams's thinking resulted in the adaptation of the psychological counseling model in which sinful, problem-centered conversations become the means of cure. Adams's psychological counseling model then became the gold standard for all the biblical counseling that followed. Mowrer was a behaviorist and past president of the American Psychological Association, and his counseling conversations influenced Adams both in content and orientation. Adams's pre- and post-Mowrer experiences led him to retrofit psychological problem-centered counseling conversations, which depended on data gathering, prying, and probing, which provoke sinful speaking, into what he named "nouthetic counseling." The word *counseling* is defined as "the provision of assistance and guidance in resolving personal, social, or psychological problems and difficulties, especially by a professional."[3] As we have indicated earlier, our concern is primarily with the sinful conversational content of biblical counseling.

Transparency

The sinful content of biblical counseling arises from Adams's exposure to the kind of counseling that calls for transparency. Self-exposure during counseling has become a psychotherapeutic necessity. Adams's use of the psychological format of transparency came out of what he experienced with O. Hobart Mowrer in 1965. The 1960s saw the rise of the encounter movement based on theories and techniques of group dynamics. The encounter movement, as experienced by Adams under Mowrer, was a huge leap into the public undressing of persons in front of as many others as happen to be in the group. One of the basic assumptions of most encounter groups is that it is emotionally beneficial to be totally transparent and open. In other words, "let it all hang out," meaning to be completely candid and straightforward, saying whatever you want and condemning whomever you wish, without any need to prove anything.

Transparency leads to deceptive feelings of intimacy, especially when the sharing majors on personal struggles with temptations and behaviors the Bible would label as sin. Such exposure can be very enticing with its focus on self. It is like a big story-telling session all about me, myself, and I and everyone else involved in my life. Sharing biased stories engenders emotional involvement in group, family, couple, and individual therapy. The therapeutic necessity of sharing personal sins and the "sins" of others is the foundation on which the sinful conversations of counseling rest, where self is center and sinful speaking of others is accepted and expected.

Learning the techniques for encouraging transparency in encounter groups influenced Adams's thinking. Thus, for Adams, self-exposure became a therapeutic absolute in the formation of his nouthetic counseling and set the gold standard for biblical counseling from *Competent to Counsel* in 1970 to this day. The biblical counseling movement (BCM) is predicated on Adams's gold standard of transparency and most all counselors today follow this same sin-saturated method of counseling.

Dr. Jay Adams's Use of the Words *Counsel* and *Counseling*

Adams brought his psychologically tainted approach into the church through his knowledge of Scripture and his ability to re-translate the New Testament according to his counseling ideas. One of the rationalizations given by Adams for using the term *counsel* is as follows:

> Because the New Testament term [*noutheteo*] is larger than the English word "counsel," and because it doesn't carry any of the "freight" that is attached to the latter term, we have simply imported the biblical term into English.[4]

In his article "What is Biblical Counseling?" Adams uses the following four verses from the Bible to describe his methodology and practice of counseling. He translates *noutheteo* uniquely here and in his own translation of the New Testament, titled *The Christian Counselor's New Testament*[5] with the words *counsel* and *counseling*, to apply these words to his system of counseling:

> Romans 15:14: "I myself am convinced about you, my brothers, that you yourselves are full of goodness, filled with all knowledge, and competent to counsel one another."
>
> 1 Thessalonians 5:12: "Now we ask you, brothers, to recognize those who labor among you, and manage you in the Lord, and counsel you."
>
> 1 Corinthians 4:14: "I am not writing these things to shame you, but to counsel you as my dear children."

> Acts 20:31: "Therefore, be alert, remembering that for three years, night and day, I didn't stop **counseling** each one of you with tears."

Adams says that the Greek verb *noutheteo* and noun *nouthesia* are "sometimes translated 'admonish, correct or instruct.'" Nevertheless, he **uniquely** chooses to translate these words as *counsel* and *counseling*. While some versions translate the Greek verb as *warn*, **we found no other version that translated *noutheteo* and *nouthesia* as *counsel* and *counseling*.** We checked these four verses with numerous versions of the English Bible, excluding amplified and paraphrased versions, and **found no support for Adams's translation of these Greek words as *counsel* and *counseling***. We also used an expository dictionary and a Greek-English lexicon and again **found no support for Adams's translation using the words *counsel* and *counseling***.[6]

The word *counsel* as used by both psychological and biblical counselors does carry a great deal of baggage. Moreover, no word translated as *counsel* in the Bible ever meant anything close to what goes on in present-day counseling where two or three people meet to talk sinfully about one person's or one couple's problems, complaints, feelings, and behavior week after week, where the focus of the conversation is the *counselee* (newly created word for the recipient of professional counseling during the 20th century) and the counselee's problems. The sinful talk involved in such a counseling process is in opposition to biblical standards of communication.

Adams also translates the following passages with *counsel* or a derivative:

noutheteo as *counseling* in Acts 20:31; Col. 1:28;

noutheteo as *counsel* Romans 15:14; 1 Cor. 4:14; Col. 3:16; 1 Thes. 5: 12,14; 2 Thes. 3:15;

nouthesia as *counseling* in Titus 3:10.

Adams says, "The three ideas found in the word *nouthesia* are **Confrontation**, **Concern**, and **Change**"[7] (emphasis his). However, **none of those words are found as translations of the word *nouthesia* in the numerous versions of the Bible we checked**. While Adams's form of counseling may include admonishment, correction, and instruction at times, there is also a great deal more that goes on in nouthetic counseling, including many unbiblical practices.

The words *counsel* and *counseling* in the biblical counseling movement resemble secular counseling, **not** what Jesus and Paul did. We think it more accurate to say that the words *noutheteo* and *nouthesia* were hijacked from the New Testament and transformed into *counsel* and *counseling* to give a biblical justification for what those who call themselves "biblical counselors" do and to avoid the obvious relationship to secular counseling with the "freight" that accompanies it.

Nouthetic Counseling

The Case of the "Hopeless" Marriage (hereafter, *The Case*) is authored by Dr. Jay E. Adams.[8] *The Case* is the *ne plus ultra* of nouthetic counseling. It is a perfect example of the nouthetic counseling approach originated by Adams. Therefore, **all who are trained to counsel nouthetically should desire to emulate this example, and all who train others in the nouthetic approach**

should hold up *The Case* as the epitome of what to copy.

The back cover of *The Case* describes the book as follows:

> *Here it is!*
>
> You've heard about Nouthetic Counseling, and wondered what it's like. People have told you all sorts of things—were they correct? Now you have the opportunity to judge for yourself. What you couldn't do before, you now can do—**peek behind the closed door to see how a typical counseling case—from beginning to end—is conducted**.
>
> In this case, which reads like a novel, Greg, a nouthetic pastor, deals with a marriage that is on the rocks. In dialog form you will read the actual exchanges that occurred, wonder what will happen next, and be confronted by evaluative analyses as the case proceeds during its ten-week duration.
>
> Written by Dr. Jay E. Adams (a pastor, counselor, and author of many books), this book is a practical illustration of God's solutions to our problems. (Bold added.)

The subtitle of *The Case* explains the contents: *A Nouthetic Counseling Case from Beginning to End*. The cover indicates that the book was written "with Greg Dawson [pastor] and Bert and Sue Lancaster [counselees]." The coauthorship is actually poetic license since *The Case* was written solely by Adams, who says: "All names and places in this book are likewise fictional and apply to no known persons walking on the face of the earth" (p. 2). According to Adams, *The Case* "is a composite based upon a number of those in which, over the years, I have counseled husbands and wives about marriages" (p. 1). However, at the conclusion of the counseling, Pastor Greg asks Bert and Sue, "Would you give permission for me to write up our counseling sessions as they have occurred in a book designed to help others learn what goes on behind closed counseling doors?" (p. 135). The (anonymous) couple agrees to have their (composite) case written up in a book that "reads like a novel."

The dialog and progression from the beginning of *The Case* to the end are all predictable and tailored to a happy conclusion. *The Case* fits the old adage, "If it sounds too good to be true, it probably is." Any psychological or biblical counselor with any experience could write a case to support whatever psychological or biblical approach they use and have a similar happy ending. And, as you read their cases, it is obvious that many have.

Adams says, "Having counseled two hours a day, two days a week, for several years, I think that I can fairly exhibit the sorts of things that husbands and wives do and say, as well as how counselors must respond" (p. 1). We approach this evaluation of *The Case* from similar experience, as we have been biblically ministering to individuals, couples, and families for over thirty-five years and have trained others to do likewise. For a number of years we headed what we called at the time "biblical counseling" at a church (we now refer to what we do and did as biblical ministry), and we have taught many to minister through classes, books we have written, correspondence, and presentations. Many others who do not use the nouthetic approach have some of the same practical experiences. **However, the true test is not personal experience, but whether or not nouthetic counseling or any other approach is truly biblical, not how many hours one has counseled or how many books one has written or how many degrees one has earned.**

Nouthetic Fundamentals

A couple, Bert and Sue, are being counseled by Pastor Greg. There are ten sessions of counseling and we select from some of the remarks made by them. Adams has Pastor Greg say the following:

> Many—perhaps most—of those who call their counseling "Christian" or even "biblical" don't really counsel according to the Scriptures.... Truly biblical counseling, in contrast, grows out of and is consistent with the Scriptures **at every point** (p. 118, bold added).

The following critique of *The Case of the "Hopeless" Marriage: A Nouthetic Counseling Case from Beginning to End* will demonstrate that **nouthetic counseling is not truly biblical "at every point."** *The Case* has a biblical façade and some biblical content, but it is not truly biblical "**at every point**." With the amount of sinful, unscriptural conversations, *The Case* is seriously flawed at many points. In addition, *The Case* reveals Adams's particular brand of Presbyterianism rather than being strictly biblical.

Throughout the nouthetic counseling case, Adams comments on the progress. After a brief interchange between Pastor Greg and the couple during the first session, Adams says:

> It looks, then, as if Greg is on track since he has begun to do the three most fundamental things that a counselor should work on in the first session: **basic data gathering**, **giving a reason to hope**, **setting the rules for counseling** (pp. 9-10, bold added).

The "**basic data gathering**" refers to Pastor Greg's use of the Personal Data Inventory (PDI), which we will discredit shortly.

"**Giving a reason to hope**" refers to Pastor Greg's following comments:

> I want you to know that **I'll work with you for as long as necessary to help you solve your problems**. And—let me say at the outset—they *can* be solved. I say that because you're both Christians. That means that you have newness of life to enable you to do God's will, you have the Bible to direct you how to do it, and you have God's Spirit to strengthen and help you do it (p. 7, italics in original, bold added).

Following this, Pastor Greg says:

> Now, let me explain a few things. I've already said that as Christians it's always possible to solve problems if you are willing to do so. But that's true only *if* you follow God's directions in His Word. No matter how bad the marriage is right now, **I *guarantee* that God will give you a marriage that sings, if you follow His directions!** But it *will* take doing what He says. I can

> say this because God has promised that (p. 8, italics in original, bold added).

Pastor Greg's promise to "**work with you for as long as necessary to help you solve your problems**" gives a false hope to the couple. What if it takes years? What if no progress is being made? What if the marriage gets worse and they file for divorce?

Another false hope is in Pastor Greg's statement: "**I *guarantee* that God will give you a marriage that sings, if you follow His directions!**" Even if they follow God at every point, further trials and tragedies may come that God will enable them to endure, but the idea of "**a marriage that sings**" is too focused on temporal enjoyment and too dependent on circumstances. Biblically speaking, what is "**a marriage that sings**"? The call of a Christian couple is not to have "**a marriage that sings**" for their mutual enjoyment, but a marriage that reflects Christ and His church (Ephesians 5).

The third most fundamental item in nouthetic counseling is "**setting the rules for counseling**." We comment on this later as we reveal the unbiblical result of one of Pastor Greg's rules for communication.

These "three most fundamental things that a counselor should work on in the first session" according to the nouthetic way are all riddled with faults. As we discuss shortly: there is no biblical need for the PDI; there is no biblical support for injecting hope in the manner done by Pastor Greg; and there is no biblical justification for communication rules that allow and even foster sinful communication.

Personal Data Inventory

Adams begins the case with Bert and Sue completing the Personal Data Inventory (PDI). The PDI requires one to list "Identification Data" (Personal), "Health Information," and "Marriage and Family Information." At the end of the PDI are six questions. At the beginning of the case, Adams presents four of the PDI questions with Bert and Sue's answers.

Pastor Greg will not only use Bert and Sue's PDI answers to guide his counseling, but he will also exercise guesses, assumptions, and opinions regarding why they answered the way they did. Adams discusses Bert and Sue's answers on the PDI. He raises questions prompted by Bert and Sue's answers that lead to guessing. For instance, Adams says:

> Note the brevity of Bert's answers. Is he embarrassed? Does he really care about the marriage—about Sue? … In response to question #2, he opens up a bit. It seems that he might want to preserve the marriage, but hasn't the faintest idea what to do….
>
> In contrast, look at Sue's more detailed responses. If she thinks there's no hope, why is she here? … Does she agree with the psychologist? She didn't take his advice, yet keeps on mentioning what he said. She probably got the idea of "incompatibility" from him….
>
> Greg is thinking well about what he read. He has used their answers productively to stimulate his thinking. He probably scribbled some of his tentative thoughts on his *Weekly Counseling*

> *Record* [a form in Adams's book *The Christian Counselor's Manual* to be used for recording counseling notes] (p. 5).

This kind of guessing and presuming are characteristic of biblical counseling and would be absent in true biblical ministry, as there is no need for it. Adams is wise in not including what Pastor Greg wrote into his notes, because there would no doubt be more obvious assumptions and opinions along with the questions that lead to guessing. Much guesswork goes on in problem-centered counseling. Besides being entirely inappropriate, such guessing and assuming have no biblical basis.

When Adams says, "Note the brevity of Bert's answers," on the PDI, he reveals that he may not be aware of two important facts. First, men in general do not want to be in counseling.[9] Second, women have special characteristics: they are more verbal and relational than men.[10] In other words, the counseling environment is more female friendly. These two facts seem to be little known to those in the biblical counseling movement, but are irrelevant when one ministers to fellow believers without doing problem-centered counseling. Men do not naturally want to participate in problem-centered counseling; they are more open to Christ-centered ministry done biblically as it does not threaten their spiritual headship.

Prior to the creation and use of the PDI Christians did minister to one another and they were in no way hampered or restricted by the non-use of the PDI. Using the PDI is entirely unnecessary as thousands of individuals who call themselves biblical counselors and others who minister biblically have never used one and could contrive equally successful cases as the one manufactured by Adams. However, the PDI and other such inventories are considered to be valuable by problem-centered counselors even though they can be a detriment when ministering biblically. Actually using the PDI could subtract from, rather than add to, the counseling process, because it will often provide distractions from the real need and provide opportunities to make unloving, unkind, and self-biased remarks about others.

Problem-Centered Nouthetic Counseling

Nouthetic counseling is a problem-centered counseling approach. **If there is no ongoing discussion of problems, there is no counseling**. Therefore, those who counsel must have problems revealed, described, and discussed in order for counseling to take place. *The Case* is a perfect example of this. Nouthetic counselors and others in the biblical counseling movement depend upon knowing problems in detail and offering solutions. Bible verses used and homework assigned are problem-centered. As Pastor Greg says: "The more I know [about the problem] the more I can help" (p. 41).

In reading *The Case*, one would think that the counselor with all his knowledge and training is the most important person in the counseling relationship. In fact, Adams poses the following near the beginning of the book: "Their marriage seems in *serious* danger at this point. If he [Pastor Greg] fails in his counseling, it will probably break up. We must await to see what he does" (emphasis his, p. 6). In other words, the success of this counseling rests significantly on the counselor. Pastor Greg's promise to work with Bert and Sue "as long as necessary to help [them] solve [their] problems" makes his role sound vital, almost as if their problems could not be solved without him. Not only is his importance exaggerated; Adams makes him sound like a real expert: "As always, Greg seems to know where he wants to go and will anticipate and lead them to those places **that breed confidence in him**" (p. 120, bold added). In fact, Pastor Greg even talks as though he can predict the future when he says of Bert's mother, "I predict that in time she'll come around" (p. 111).

Scientific research evidence diminishes the importance of the counselor and the counselor's training, experience, and methods. According to the research, the most important human elements in change are Bert and Sue and their desire to change.[11] Worse than that, Pastor Greg works to "**breed confidence in him**," that is, in himself. A truly biblical ministry would always be to encourage greater confidence in the Lord. **This exaggerated importance of the counselor and his expertise reflects the theories and practices of secular psychotherapy, diminishes the role of the Holy Spirit, and discourages ordinary members of the Body of Christ from ministering to one another.**

The assumption in *The Case* is that Bert and Sue are Christians, since they had "joined the 'First Scriptural Presbyterian Church' two years ago." Adams further says, "Both were converted under the evangelistic efforts of one of the church's elders" (p. 2). Pastor Greg also refers to them as "both Christians" (p. 7). However, the fact that Bert and Sue are members of the church is no guarantee that they are true believers. Sometimes it's helpful to ignore the fact that they are church members and ask about their relationship with the Lord. At other times whether or not they are saved will become apparent as one ministers.

Bert and Sue come to Pastor Greg for help because their marriage is falling apart (p. 1). Bert and Sue describe their problems in the PDI and then Pastor Greg discusses their problems with them. He asks questions about the problems, because, as a nouthetic counselor, he must gather data about the problems, which is unnecessary when one is truly biblical. The PDI and questions that follow provide many opportunities for Bert and Sue to say hurtful things about each other in front of a third party. And, indeed the PDI and questions bring forth self-biased, unloving, sinful remarks along with blaming the spouse, justifying self, and expressing anger, all of which are sinful according to the Scriptures (Prov. 11:13; 15:1; 18:17; 27:15; 29:22; Eph. 4:29). Providing a venue for such husband-wife interchange militates against a biblical marital relationship (Eph. 5:22-33).

The following are the types of problems surfaced by the couple (pp. 71, 105, 114):

> Bert: Does not pick up his socks.
>
> Does not take out the trash regularly.
>
> Sue: Unloads on Bert as soon as he comes home from work.
>
> Does not serve meals that please Bert.

When the pastor asks Bert to tell him about the main problem in their marriage, Bert replies, "Well, we haven't been getting along for some time now. It seems that she won't let me be the head of the house. I..." At that point Sue interrupts Bert and says, "Won't let you. When did you ever try? You know full well that you..."

The pastor then interrupts Sue and asks her to let Bert finish what he was saying. Then Bert says, "Well, as I was saying—before she flew into one of her tirades…" Sue interrupts again and says, "See, pastor, he can't be civil. A tirade? Hummph!" (p. 11). Instead of bringing truth and love into the conversation, the counselor ends up being a kind of referee whose rules allow a great deal of sinful speaking between the husband and wife In addition to the problems they are already experiencing with each other come the wounds of criticism that are bound to sink way down (Prov. 26:22).

The pastor invites Bert to continue even though he is speaking ill about his wife and exposing her faults to a third party. Bert then says, "As I was saying, every time I try to assume my duty as the head of my home, Sue undermines me. She always knows better. She always has another way. She always contradicts me. The kids don't know who to believe" (p. 12).

The pastor does set some restrictions on their rude and hurtful communication, such as having them speak to him instead of to each other and telling them not to exaggerate. Thus they are allowed to speak ill of one another as long as they do not speak directly to each other. Not being allowed to speak to one another during counseling is an artificial restriction that does not prevent the sinful talk, but merely keeps things somewhat under the pastor's control. He thereby maintains his authoritative position, rather than being reduced to the sidelines during any argument that might erupt. One can easily see how the problem-centeredness of the counseling opens the door to couples breaking God's commandments to husbands and wives in Ephesians 5:22-33 and 1 Peter 3:5-10.

When the pastor attempts to teach Bert about loving his wife, he responds, "It's just that if she'd listen to me, I could love her more." Then when the pastor gives biblical instruction regarding the husband to love his wife, Sue remarks, "See, I told him! He should love me by putting me first" (p. 15). This sinful talk could have been avoided if the pastor had cautioned them at the beginning about how speaking ill of one another and exposing each other's faults are the very opposite of love and respect.

At the end of the first session, Pastor Greg assigns homework. He says:

> Each of you is to compose a list of 100 or more ways that you are failing God as a person, as a husband or wife, and as a father or mother.… Write out your lists, and when you've finished draw a line and then hand the lists to one another to add anything that may be missing. **List specific things that bother you about one another** (p. 21, bold added).

This is a long list of 200 possible problems the couple has as "a person, as a husband or wife, and as a father or mother." Add this to problems already revealed in the PDI and the problems already discussed and the problem-centered counselor has the usual pile of problems to serve as fodder for future problem-centered counseling sessions riddled with sinful speaking. However, the mere listing of their gripes and failings could easily make matters worse. Listing 100 or more ways each for Bert and Sue to change is a negative and unnecessary assignment, but it does give the nouthetic counselor something to talk about for the upcoming sessions. We wonder how many couples would actually do the assignment and how many might fail to return for more counseling. But, when one contrives a case, one can make the imaginary couple do anything.

It would have been far better to suggest to Bert and Sue that each one bring back a list of items for which they are thankful to the Lord. These can be a springboard away from problem-centeredness to Christ-centeredness. Moving them from their thanksgiving list to prayer, the Word, and worship would encourage them to grow spiritually, draw closer to the Lord, and thereby, in most cases, enable them to deal with their problems on their own.

Although the pastor has given some good instruction along the way, the problem-centeredness of biblical counseling with its sinful speaking comes out again when Sue says to Bert, "You've never done much disciplining, Bert—I've had it all on my shoulders. You know that. Don't make it sound like you have!" Instead of helping Sue, Pastor Greg is enabling her to be a foolish woman who tears down her house (Prov. 14:1). It appears as though the whole marital relationship must be torn down in order to solve marriage problems in biblical counseling.

In response, Bert says, "Now, Sue, you know how hard I've tried, but to be honest, you also know that you always contradict what I tell them [the children] and they get confused. In time, I finally gave up" (p. 75). Whoops! Here they are breaking Pastor Greg's rule. They are speaking to each other here instead of complaining about each other to the pastor. Worse than that, this kind of counseling majors in such self-justifying, blame-shifting remarks, as though such arguments must happen in front of the counselor so that he can save their marriage. Or, is it because many in the church assume that this kind of talk is okay and even necessary in the counseling room?

There is no biblical example in Scripture of this type of counseling as practiced in *The Case*. Such repeated airing of complaints about each other and ongoing discussions about problems of living during numerous counseling sessions as in *The Case* have no precedence in Scripture. This one-week-after-another, one-to-one or one-to-two in this case, one-appointment-after-another (p. 39), and the **one-up of Pastor Greg** are all part of biblical counseling.[12] Examples of this can be seen throughout *The Case*. In Galatians 6:1-3 the apostle Paul speaks of the necessary humility on the part of the one who ministers, which would abrogate the one-up/one-down approach of nouthetic counseling.

The Case gives the impression that it's as easy as falling off a log to transform a troubled marriage when, in reality, it is one of the most difficult areas to deal with because of problem-centeredness, in which couples say hurtful things about each other in front of a third party. **With certain exceptions, it is sinful to discuss marital problems with others or to complain about one's spouse to someone in each other's presence or absence (Eph. 5:21, 22, 25; Prov. 18:17).** She talks about him when he's not there; he talks about her when she's not there; or they talk about one another in front of the counselor. **In problem-centered counseling biblical counselors not only listen to ongoing complaints, but often encourage such expression.** Personal or marital problem-centered counseling encourages one to expose sins, secrets, and private matters of others and is often dependent on talebearing. In contrast, there are biblical ways to deal with personal failings and sinfulness without exposing the failures or sins of others. Those who minister biblically do not need to know specifics about the problems or to necessarily offer solutions directly related to the problems.

External Behavior

Nouthetic counseling invariably leads to working on external behavior (the "problem") and ends up being a program of works (do's and don't's). At the encouragement of Pastor Greg to prepare a list of ways that Bert could give himself to Sue (p. 55), Bert comes up with the following:

1. Fix broken vacuum cleaner handle.
2. Spend time with the kids on Saturday so Sue can be freed up.
3. Clear the table after meals.
4. Take Sue out for dinner once a month while having a baby sitter stay with the boys (p. 57).

Bert's list is a characteristic result of nouthetic counseling and other problem-centered approaches. The counselees are encouraged to write such lists and then encouraged to follow them. There is no precedence for this in the Bible or, for that matter, in the past history of ministry in the church. It is a result of following the practices of the secular psychological counseling movement, which is problem-centered. The do's and don't's and should's and ought's in *The Case* are heavily behaviorally oriented. Nouthetic counseling strongly emphasizes external behavior.

Adams trusts that as counselees change their external behavior, they will also change their attitudes and other aspects of their internal selves. He has Pastor Greg saying such things as this: "You know, Bert, great changes in attitudes can result from small changes in behavior" (p. 45). He repeats the same idea later: "You see, just as I said when discussing the socks, large changes in attitudes can take place over small changes in behavior" (p. 47). Consequently there is much teaching having to do with external behavior and rules to follow. For Adams, spiritual growth appears to be more dependent on what one **does** than on faith in Christ working **in** the believer.

Adams has been consistent in promoting this idea of external change leading to internal change. In his book *Competent to Counsel* he says, "God sets forth the important principle that behavior determines feelings.... People feel bad because of bad behavior; feelings flow from actions."[13] There appears to be far more emphasis on what one is to do in nouthetic counseling than on the very life of Christ in the believer.

Throughout his methodology, Adams has stressed changing behavior and habits as a means of inner change and spiritual growth. However, all the external change that Bert and Sue make could be done in the flesh just by believing that their circumstances would improve and they would have a "marriage that sings" if they made these small changes. While problems may be solved and counselees may develop new habits, there may be no true spiritual growth, even when an interest is being shown in knowing more of the Bible. The Pharisees were experts in Scripture and in external behavior as well.

Scripture teaches about believers working out (through obedience) what God is working in them: "For it is God which worketh in you both to will and to do of his good pleasure" (Phil. 2: 13). Good works (external) follow faith (internal) (Eph. 2:8-10) for salvation and also for sanctification. However, Adams seems to reverse the order this way: as believers follow God's commandments on the outside, they will change on the inside. Adams appears to be committed to the idea that righteousness comes from obeying the law, for he declares: "Liberty comes through the law, not apart from it."[14] The epistle to the Galatians teaches the opposite: "Stand fast therefore in the liberty wherewith Christ hath made us free, and be not entangled again with the yoke of bondage" (Gal. 5:1) and is confirmed in Romans:

> For the law of the Spirit of life in Christ Jesus hath made me free from the law of sin and death. For what the law could not do, in that it was weak through the flesh, God sending his own Son in the likeness of sinful flesh, and for sin, condemned sin in the flesh: That the righteousness of the law might be fulfilled in us, who walk not after the flesh, but after the Spirit (Romans 8:2-4).

Scripture clearly teaches that, though the law is holy and has great purposes and effects, it cannot make one holy. Not even the moral law can make one righteous. The believer who is living the new life in Christ will express the law of the Spirit through external obedience, but does not establish or even develop the inner life through the correction of external behavior. One becomes holy through what Christ has already accomplished and continues to work in the believer throughout the process of sanctification. The holiness comes from Christ. It is expressed through holy living, not the other way around. If one attempts to become holy by behavior, one merely cleans up the outside (Matt. 23:25), but if one becomes holy by faith in the finished work of Christ, the resulting change in behavior will be an expression of the holy life within.

Bert can be encouraged to pick up his socks or to pick up his Bible. Nouthetic counseling, while not ignoring the Bible would emphasize Bert picking up his socks, while biblical ministry would emphasize Bert picking up the Bible, without ignoring needed changes in his outward behavior.

Discussing Marital Problems

Bert and Sue argue, exhibit anger towards one another, and heap blame on one another all in Pastor Greg's presence. While he sets up rules for them not to speak directly to each other, he allows and even encourages them to talk about each other and to express their frustration with each other to him. He ends up being a kind of referee to enable them to talk sinfully about what's wrong with each other and to expose each other's failings so that he will have something to work with in this problem-centered environment.

Discussing marital problems in one another's presence to a third party is unbiblical. Originally, this kind of counseling was the psychological way, but now, by copy-catting, it is the so-called biblical way of counseling. In addition, the problem-centered approach taken in biblical counseling tends to corrupt the biblical roles of both men and women, and particularly in marital counseling.[15] Pastor Greg corrupts Bert's spiritual headship by eliciting and discussing problems in the marriage and then leading the couple to solutions. Pastor Greg corrupts Sue's role by having her submit to himself rather than to her husband. In contrast, true biblical ministry will encourage Bert and Sue to grow biblically and thus spiritually. In that way Bert will learn to obey the Lord in exercising his spiritual headship in love, and Sue will learn to submit to Bert "as unto the Lord" (Eph. 5:22-33).

Pastor Greg's counseling encourages the couple to sin in order to save their marriage. Pastor Greg is in the process of "establishing rules: no interruptions, no **nasty** talk" (bold added), but "nasty talk" is already condoned and encouraged by Pastor Greg, who is only curbing against exaggeration and the two speaking directly to one another (pp. 11-13). Adams says: "You will notice that Pastor Greg has established God's Word as the standard for what will go on in counseling" (p. 13). And yet, God's standard is violated all over the place in the problem-centered structure in which counselees are free to discard many admonitions regarding how **Christians are to speak and conduct themselves in truth and love (I Cor. 13:4-8; Eph. 4:15, 29; Col. 4:6; James 3:2-8; Titus 3:2).** Counseling sessions that are made up of cruel and demeaning remarks about spouses, parents, and others fall far short of the mark, and yet it seems that no one cares. Pastor Greg has allowed and even encouraged, throughout the PDI and subsequent conversations, unedifying statements to be made by the couple about each other (see Eph. 4:29). **Pastor Greg's counseling sessions are full of murmuring, complaining, not showing love to the wife, and dishonoring the husband (Prov. 12:4; 15:1; Eph. 5:33).**

Although Pastor Greg does not allow them to say these "nasty" things **to each other**, they are directed to say these same things to him **about each other**. This is a violation of Ephesians 5. Bert refers to Sue flying "into one of her tirades" (p. 11). Sue says of Bert, "He blew off steam at his boss yesterday, saying a few choice words, and the boss fired him. Disgusting, isn't it?" (p. 23). Some of the most petty things are said, such as Sue saying, "I think the second thing is his socks. He throws them on the floor at night, and I have to put them in the hamper the next morning" (p. 36).

It is unfortunate and unbiblical that Pastor Greg in "establishing rules" says "no **nasty** talk." The word *nasty* is deplorable because the first definition of the word nasty is "physically filthy, disgustingly unclean." Like many words, the word *nasty* has less extreme meanings, but why use such a word when it could be misunderstood? Why does Pastor Greg avoid calling such talk "sinful"? It would have been more biblically correct for Pastor Greg to say, "no sinful talk." **However, the words "sin" and "sinful" are almost totally absent in *The Case*!** Pastor Greg does advise Bert to use the word *sin* when apologizing to his boss (p. 30) and Adams refers to this as sin in his discussion (p. 32). Pastor Greg does once refer to sin in a general way when he says, "Our sinful ways make us incompatible with God" (p. 63).

Aside from these instances, the words "sin" and "sinful" seem totally absent from the ten sessions in *The Case,* in spite of the fact that there are **numerous instances during the counseling where sin could be called *sin,* but was not**. In addition, Adams has an Appendix in which he lists "Some of the More Notable Ways in which Greg Brought This Case to a Successful End" (pp. 137-142). Out of the 100 items listed by Adams, only one mentions "sinners" (#99). If one looks up the word *sin* and all of its variations in the Bible, it is certainly a major biblical doctrine and needs to be identified as such when necessary. **Based upon Adams's ideal example, exemplified in *The Case*, nouthetic counseling seems to be an almost "sinless" approach.** This serious omission of the word *sin* is one possible result of problem-centered counseling. Problem-centered counselors become so problem-centered that they oftentimes ignore the sinfulness of the counseling conversations.

Adams's list of 100 of "Some of the More Notable Ways in which Greg Brought This Case to a Successful End" reveals just how one-up (Pastor Greg) is and two-down (Bert and Sue) are and how problem-centered nouthetic counseling is. Unfortunately many will read the list as something to emulate and read it over and over again to obtain some gems for biblical counseling. Others will be intimidated, overwhelmed, and discouraged. Christ-centered ministry has no such complex, convoluted lists to follow, because no such lists are needed to minister.

The details and the drama of Bert and Sue are brought out in nouthetic counseling. If Bert truly loved his wife as Christ loved the church and gave Himself for her

(Eph. 5:25) and if Sue were submissive to her husband and honored him (Eph. 5:24), they would not be sharing their marital problems with a third party. It is entirely unnecessary and unbiblical to share their marital problems with a third party. There is a better way, a biblical way that does not require this public airing of problems, but surely resolves them if they are resolvable.

Dishonoring Mother

Another problem that comes up has to do with Bert's mother. Sue begins with, "You see, Bert's mother lives two blocks away from us. So she's always coming over to our house. When she does, she is always trying to run our lives. She comes over and tells Bert what to think and do; and most of the time he listens to her…." Sue adds, "She's a Charismatic who is always getting a 'prophetic word' to reinforce what she tells us to do" (p. 92). Of course Bert's mother is not present to say whether or not she is trying to run their lives. Bert's mother's intent is assumed and believed. Here again they are encouraged to dishonor Bert's mother by speaking ill of her behind her back and placing her in the worst light.

Pastor Greg rightly refers to Genesis 2:24, "Therefore shall a man leave his father and his mother, and cleave unto his wife: and they shall be one flesh." He asks, "Why do you suppose there are no mother-in-law jokes about the woman's mother-in-law?" (p. 93). Regardless of the point he is trying to make, he is in error. We did an internet search for mother-in-law jokes and found such jokes about the husband's mother-in-law **and** about the wife's mother-in-law. So Greg's use of the word "no," meaning "not one," is false, which injects an added negative about Bert's mother, prior to suggesting that Bert go to his mother and basically telling him what to say. It is very easy to "write a script" for someone else, but the script may not at all fit within the context of their relationship. Nevertheless Pastor Greg says:

> … tell her in a kindly way that you are the head of a new family. Also tell her that, while happy to hear her suggestions, you will make your own decisions and not be persuaded to act as she wants simply because of who she is. And assure her that you will no longer allow any undue pressure or influence to interfere with your home life (p. 93).

Pastor Greg's suggested words carry a pretty hot criticism of Bert's mother by indirectly accusing her of aggressively interfering in Bert's life and then having Bert tell her that he will "no longer allow" his mother to put pressure on him. What kind of authority is a son to take over his mother to say he would "not allow" her to do something. Instead of this unwise suggested pronouncement, Bert could simply proceed with doing what is right.

Bert rightly asks, "Wouldn't that hurt her?" Pastor Greg says:

> She shouldn't be hurt if she handles what you say as a Christian should. We don't act on the basis of whether others take offense at what we do, but on the basis of whether or not it is what God wants us to do (pp. 93-94).

We agree with Pastor Greg that one should act "on the basis of whether or not it is what God wants us to do." However, we disagree with what he thinks God would want Bert to do. Is Greg attempting to change their circumstances by changing Bert's mother? We would also ask: why does Bert even have to tell his mother any of this, since these are his decisions for his own behavior change? Then, if she asks why he is not doing things her way, he could gently explain his responsibilities to lead his family without any implied criticism of his mother. We respect Bert's concern about the possibility of hurting his mother and would suggest that he pray about these needed changes and about how to accomplish his goal to be the head of the household in a way that would be pleasing to God and least hurtful to his mother. These are matters for drawing close to God, praying, and seeking God's wisdom.

At the next appointment, Bert tells Pastor Greg that he went to his mother and told her that, "while I would welcome advice, I would no longer allow anyone to meddle in our private affairs." Bert then says that his mother "told me off in non-Charismatic terms" (p. 102).

The commandment is clear: "Honour thy father and thy mother" (Exodus 20:12). There was no need for Bert to confront his mother as bluntly as he did. Not only do problem-centered counselors often permit their counselees to dishonor their mothers and fathers; they often encourage and participate in the process. Those who follow Freudian psychological notions will dishonor their mothers and fathers by blaming them for their current problems. It is sinful to do so.

Non-Nouthetic Problems

There are several problems unrelated to biblical counseling that need to be noted, as they are serious distractions from *The Case* itself, **but are normal outcomes of problem-centered counseling. There is a misrepresentation of Dr. James Dobson's position on divorce, the promotion of the Presbyterian Church versus the caricature of all Charismatics, and the implied denigration of the role of women in the church.**

Dr. James Dobson

In reply to one of the questions on the PDI, Sue says:

> I didn't think that divorce was a possibility until a friend recently gave me a copy of an old article by Dr. James Dobson entitled, "Husband Who Feels Suffocated Needs To Be Set Free." He says that I can "open the cage door" and let my husband go free!!! Maybe that's the best thing to do. I've attached a copy of the article to this Inventory (p. 4).

This article by Dobson is repeatedly referred to throughout *The Case* with Pastor Greg and Sue believing that Dobson is recommending divorce (pp. 5, 49, 51, 54, 55, 63, 66). Pastor Greg claims that Dobson advises "the opposite of what God says in the Bible" (p. 55).

However, we obtained and read a copy of Dobson's article, "Husband Who Feels Suffocated Needs To Be Set Free."[16] Contrary to what Pastor Greg and the couple believed, the article does **not** advise divorce. If Sue and Pastor Greg think that the article supports divorce, Adams, himself, must have misunderstood Dobson's article; otherwise he would not have made such an erroneous issue of it! To further check this out, we called Focus on the Family and were told that the article does **not** advise divorce. We were told to visit a web site to see Dobson's views on divorce.[17] We read Dobson's views on divorce by reading his articles on "Relationships" on that site. We conclude that Dobson's view is the same as Adams's view, which is "that there are only two legitimate reasons for believers to divorce, and then, there is no necessity to do so" (p. 51).

As our readers know, we have authored a book and many articles critical of Dobson.[18] However, here we must come to Dobson's defense. His views on divorce have been misrepresented throughout *The Case.* Problem-centered counseling often results in comments about what the counselee says, such as about Dobson, that end up to be false, just as this one is.

Presbyterians versus Charismatics

Adams refers at the beginning to the fact that Bert and Sue joined the "First Scriptural Presbyterian Church." Adams is Presbyterian and thus links *The Case* at the beginning to a Presbyterian church. Pastor Greg, the counselor in *The Case*, is obviously a Presbyterian pastor.

Bert's mother is a Charismatic, and, just as all Presbyterians are not the same, not all Charismatics are the same. Bert's mother, Mrs. Brown (her different last name is not explained), is a Charismatic who was earlier described as using a so-called "prophetic word" to support her advice to Bert and Sue (p. 92). During the special counseling session that included Bert's mother, she said to Pastor Greg, "Alright! I just received a word of knowledge telling me not to listen to anything you say… that you don't understand the Bible…that you are of the devil" (p. 110).

Pastor Greg refers to what he calls "the Charismatic problem" (p. 94). Adams's comments refer to the "Charismatic issue" (p. 95). Note that this is not just dealing specifically with Mrs. Brown, but with **all charismatics**. Pastor Greg recommends Adams's two books having to do with charismatics: *The Christian's Guide to Guidance* and *Signs and Wonders in the Last Days*.

Bert later says that he read the two books and then says, "I wish every Charismatic—including Mom—would read them!" (p. 122).

Pastor Greg responds, "Who knows? Perhaps the time will come when she will be willing—after she comes to recognizes [sic] the good 'Presbyterianism' has done for her and you" (p. 122). Later, Pastor Greg says of Bert's mother: "There's still a long way to go, but we're going to persist until we win her over completely—and I hope that even means to become a member of Scriptural Pres" [his church!] (p. 132).

Although Pastor Greg cautions against "exaggeration" and "overstatement" (pp. 12, 92), it is obvious that he (therefore Adams), by characterizing **all** charismatics according to the fictional character of Bert's mother, is guilty of both exaggeration and overstatement. Are there charismatics like Bert's mother? Yes. But there are other charismatics who would be in agreement with Adams's criticisms of her, even though they would obviously disagree with his generalization describing all charismatics. The exalting of Presbyterians and the demeaning of charismatics through caricature and generalization are entirely uncalled for and distract from whether or not nouthetic counseling, per se, is biblical. Presbyterian parochialism is transparent throughout *The Case*. Adams must be aware that his own Presbyterian denomination is accused of being legalistic, a generalization he would probably deny. We need to be careful about generalizing about other denominations. **Problem-centered counseling easily leads to such talk**.

Role of Women

Adams refers to "the flawed teaching in many women's Bible studies" (p. 66). Pastor Greg says, "Some women's study groups are an opportunity to meet and pool ignorance as they fill in white space in booklets that ask questions but provide no answers" (p. 55). This, of course, is obviously true of some study groups of men, women, or couples. This is even true of some study groups led by pastors, elders, and other church leaders.

Sue later asks Pastor Greg, "Pastor, do you have a good women's Bible study group I can attend?" (p. 117). In response, Pastor Greg says, "So glad you asked. No, at the moment we don't. I know that there are one or two women who from time to time have expressed the same desire, but we've never had enough to form a group" (p. 117). He then encourages Sue to gather a group and says, "I'll get an elder to teach it. If I can't find one whose schedule is open, I'll teach it myself" (p. 118). Only "one or two women" in Pastor Greg's church "from time to time have expressed the same desire" for a "women's Bible study group"? How sad!

What comes across is that Pastor Greg is critical of "some women's study groups" and apparently does not encourage women in his church to become involved in one; but if they are interested either an elder or he himself will teach the class. Why not a woman to teach the class? This is more a reflection of Adams's particular Presbyterian orientation than a biblical mandate.

Bert and Sue in Christ-Centered Ministry

The Case is a clear example of a problem-centered biblical counseling system and typical counselor-counselee relationship. Here we present a few ways of ministering to Bert and Sue in Christ-centered ministry. An overall difference is that we would emphasize the work of Christ in Bert and Sue **rather than focus on the specific problems they are experiencing.** Bert and Sue could be ministered to biblically without sinful communication and tale bearing that assume another's intent or heart attitude. **Problem-centered counseling, however, thrives on and even encourages such sinful communication.**

When people like Bert and Sue are experiencing such marital problems as they discuss, there is clearly something amiss in their walk with the Lord. Therefore we would emphasize how problems of living can actually be turned into opportunities for spiritual growth. We would want to help them see their situation from God's perspective. Their problems are a wake-up call to walk according to the Spirit rather than according to the flesh. Problem-centered counselors may contend that working on behavior will result in walking according to the Spirit. Yet, we believe that people can make all kinds of external changes while continuing to walk according to the flesh and even strengthening it by doing so. After all, in problem-centered counseling the sinful flesh is given ample opportunity to express itself through gripes, complaints, and sinful conversations about one another and about people not present. Therefore, while ministering to Bert and Sue, rather than having to rely on such sinful, fleshly conversation in order to figure out what to counsel, we would be teaching and reminding them **that problems of living are opportunities for spiritual growth and change**.

It is clear from the description of Bert and Sue that they have no clue as to the real source of their problems, which is their own flesh and spiritual wickedness in high places (Eph. 6:12). They are each wanting the other person to change. They are struggling against each other instead of donning their spiritual armor, standing firm in faith, praying, and seeking God's will. As they grow spiritually, they will better know how to handle problems by grace through faith, prayer, worship, praise, thanksgiving, and obedience, and they will thereby be glorifying God and fulfilling His purposes. Yes, there are biblical admonitions for what they can do about certain specific problems, but they need to see the larger picture so that they will discover for themselves what they can do about their problems that would please God rather than self and Satan.

Prayer is an essential part of every meeting and should be done whenever appropriate. We might ask Bert and Sue what help they are seeking from the Lord, because that would show us a general area in which He may be working in their lives. We would want to know enough to participate in what God is doing. When fellow believers, such as Bert and Sue, share problems, there is room for briefly hearing the general concern, as long as their description does not violate Scripture. However we would quickly redirect the conversation and attention away from their problems and onto Christ and all He has provided. A concerted effort generally needs to be made to draw attention to Christ Himself, because counselees like Bert and Sue will almost always drift back into the direction of talking about their problems. If Bert and Sue are only looking for immediate solutions, they will miss the great opportunity to know Christ better and to grow spiritually.

Since Bert and Sue are presented as professing believers, we would encourage them to talk about their relationship with the Lord. Together Bert and Sue and the ministering couple could talk about the riches of what has been included in the death, burial, and resurrection of Christ and by our identification with Him. Some Christians have an incomplete understanding of redemption, why it was necessary and all it entails. We would want to make sure that Bert and Sue have a clear understanding and ongoing gratitude for God's most precious gift. We would desire to help Bert and Sue see the utter sinfulness of the flesh, gaze at the perfections of Jesus Christ, and desire to reflect Him.

We may also ask Bert and Sue to talk about the blessings they have already received in Christ Jesus, such as God's immeasurable love, salvation, new life, imputed righteousness, freedom from the law of sin and death, eternal life, and "all spiritual blessings in heavenly places in Christ" (Eph. 1:3). When attention is given to the magnificent love relationship that God has given every believer in Christ, there is a great opportunity for gratitude to flow and for the desire to do His will to increase.

We would encourage Bert and Sue to look to Jesus in every trial, just as Jesus invites them in Matthew 11:28-30.

> Come unto me, all ye that labour and are heavy laden, and I will give you rest. Take my yoke upon you, and learn of me; for I am meek and lowly in heart: and ye shall find rest unto your souls. For my yoke is easy, and my burden is light.

How much better it is to help fellow believers grow in their walk with the Lord than to focus on the problem itself, for, as they yoke themselves with Christ in this problem and seek to follow Him through this trial, they will be prepared to face future difficulties. Moreover, they will learn to walk according to their new life in Christ, rather than according to the old ways of the flesh.

The conversation with Bert and Sue might include something like this: "In your circumstances there are some things you can do to grow spiritually, which may, in the long run, change the circumstances as well. What changes might Jesus plan to work in you through these circumstances?" If Bert and Sue talk about interpersonal problems or complain about each other or about other people, we would redirect the conversation away from how their spouse or others need to change to what Christ would want them to do and to how Christ can use their problems to bring about their own spiritual growth.

However, **more than working on specific issues**, we would desire to help Bert and Sue "comprehend with all the saints what is the breadth, and length, and depth, and height; and to know the love of Christ, which passeth knowledge, that [they] might be filled with all the fullness of God" (Eph. 3:18-19), for it is out of this great love relationship that the new life flows. Thus, Bert and Sue should come to that place of praying something like this: "Lord, I want to know you better and love you more through this problem. Use me to accomplish your will in this situation." Indeed, Ephesians 3:20 applies to such a prayer for it says, "Now unto Him that is able to do exceeding abundantly above all that we ask or think, according to the power that worketh in us."

We would confront Bert and Sue with God's great love and redemptive power as we attempt to encourage their love for God so that there would be an outflowing of Christ's life. After all, the problem is not only that Bert is not loving his wife as Christ loves the church, but moreover that he is not living according to his new life in Christ, through which He would receive God's love and be able to love God enough to love his wife and to surmount problems even if circumstances do not change. As Bert and Sue's behavior is presented in *The Case*, it is clear that they had reverted to the flesh, and much of the effort they are making through counseling appears to be primarily works, motivated by the pastor's promise that their marriage will "sing." But, what if such a couple's marriage never sings? Will they still grow spiritually by grace through faith?

As Bert and Sue truly respond to God's love for them, they will love Him and desire to do His will. As they walk in this love relationship by grace through faith according to the new life He has given them, the Holy Spirit will enable them to love and obey Him more and more. Therefore all personal ministry should nurture that love for God. Bert and Sue will also show forth their love for God by loving one another and forgiving one another. We may also remind Bert and Sue that, because of His great love for them, God may even allow problems to build and fester to further conform them to the image of Christ. In love He will discipline them as they need it (Heb. 12:11). Therefore, they should not automatically expect things to be rosy right away, because they may need more tribulation to bring forth patience, experience, hope, and love (Romans 5:3-5).

When people like Bert and Sue are going through problems of living **they need to be encouraged to turn to God and worship Him daily.** People like Bert and Sue, who have been focused on their problems, definitely need a new perspective. They may need to be instructed about worship and about how they might worship God on a daily basis along with daily prayer and Bible reading. Bert and Sue need to learn or to remember that problems are calls to worship, for worship has to do with our recognition and submission to God's greatness, perfection, power, sovereignty, and authority over all His creation. They would be worshipping God when they place themselves under His authority and power and when they sanctify Him in their hearts (1 Peter 3:15) in meekness and holy fear. What better place is there to be when we are suffering?

Those who minister need to lead fellow believers into Christ-honoring conversations, rather than encouraging ongoing complaints and expressions of bitterness. Although such sinful conversations may expose what counselors may be looking for in order to "understand the counselees and their problems," the damage that can occur may lead troubled marriages right into divorce court. Too often couples are more interested in changing their spouse and erroneously think that "telling on the other" will bring about desired change. The encouragement must be for spiritual growth for each one present, including the person who is ministering. Confessing one's own sins may bring true repentance and spiritual growth. Confessing another person's sins aggravates the situation and fosters pride, self-protection, and bitterness.

If a couple will not be open to the prior suggestions and the conversation deteriorates as in *The Case*, they need to be ministered to separately with a man ministering to the husband and a woman ministering to the wife regarding what Christ has provided for the Christian life and how to grow in Him. If a similar conversation occurs as with *The Case*-type Bert/Sue during individual ministry and is carried on unabated by both the husband and wife, that ministry needs to cease, for the spiritual good of both. Continually resorting to the flesh when discussing conflicts in the presence of a third party will only serve to exacerbate the problem and work against Ephesians 4:31-32, "Let all bitterness, and wrath, and anger, and clamour, and evil speaking, be put away from you, with all malice: and be ye kind one to another, tenderhearted, forgiving one another, even as God for Christ's sake hath forgiven you." Ministry can then continue if and when one or both are ready to speak kindly to and about one other. God's love must continually be front and center in order to help a husband and wife love each other according to 1 Corinthians 13:4-7:

> Charity suffereth long, and is kind; charity envieth not; charity vaunteth not itself, is not puffed up, doth not behave itself unseemly, seeketh not

> her own, is not easily provoked, thinketh no evil; rejoiceth not in iniquity, but rejoiceth in the truth; beareth all things, believeth all things, hopeth all things, endureth all things.

Love should be the goal of all personal ministry: loving God and one another. Those who minister to couples need to protect them from the sin-saturated counseling conversations as revealed in *The Case*! which are tremendously unloving and unkind. **With all the sinful speaking enabled in *The Case*, it is apparent that *The Case of the "Hopeless" Marriage* is actually a case of hopeless counseling.**

3

Dr. David Powlison

The Christian Counseling & Education Foundation (CCEF) website describes Dr. David Powlison as follows:

> David Powlison serves as CCEF's executive director, as a faulty member, and as senior editor of the *Journal of Biblical Counseling*. He holds a PhD from the University of Pennsylvania and an MDiv from Westminster Theological Seminary. David has written extensively on biblical counseling and on the relationship between faith and psychology.[1]

In a 2003 *PsychoHeresy Awareness Letter* we reveal that several counselors at CCEF have been longtime members of the American Association of Christian Counselors (AACC), Dr. John Bettler (Executive Director of CCEF at the time) since 6/24/91 and Powlison since 1/11/93.[2] The AACC is committed to the integration of psychology and the Bible. In addition, CCEF has been a fellow traveler with many integrationists through recommending their books or endorsing their work. One in particular that we have exposed over the years is Leslie Vernick, who is a psychologically trained, licensed counselor in private practice, whose books are offered by CCEF, and who has taught for them. [3] And, last but not least, is the fact that Powlison endorses Dr. Eric L. Johnson's book *Foundations for Soul Care*, which promotes integration.[4]

CCEF is a separated-from-the-church biblical counseling center, which charges fees for its counseling services, which means its counselees are "clients," just like its psychotherapy counterparts. In Chapter 9 we describe these two unbiblical practices.[5] In 2015 CCEF's gross receipts were $3,752,075. The "Home Office" of CCEF has 15 counselors plus interns in addition to Powlison, who is the executive director. CCEF's counseling fee is $95 per hour. Because these appointments are not generally covered by insurance, the website says: "All counseling charges are due prior to each appointment."[6] This one serious violation of Scripture and its pharisaical justification[7] should be enough for all to turn away from the "cash, check, or credit-card" mentality of CCEF and others who purvey passion for pay and compassion for cash.

Dr. Heath Lambert, in his PhD dissertation, turned into a book titled *The Biblical Counseling Movement after Adams*, says that Powlison is "the clear leader" of the "second generation of biblical counselors." [8] Lambert says:

> It would be difficult to overstate the influence of Powlison's contribution has had on biblical counselors. Indeed it could be fair to say that over the last twenty years the movement has been defined by the usage of Powlison's metaphor. The "idols of the heart" metaphor has been used extensively by any number of authors.[9]

In contrast to Adams' "behavioristic" nouthetic counseling, Powlison's "idols-of-the-heart" (IOTH) counseling is still nouthetic, but "psychoanalytic." We put *psychoanalytic* in quotes because his IOTH counseling includes two important central concepts that are reflective of the Freudian unconscious and insight.

Psychology professor Dr. Paul Vitz was an invited speaker at CCEF. The advertisement in the 1988 CCEF publication *Pulse* says:

> CCEF is extremely pleased to announce that Dr. Vitz will offer a two-day seminar entitled, "Christianity and Psychology: An Insider's View.[10]

Four years earlier Vitz had written two articles for the *Journal of Psychology and Theology* titled "Christianity and Psychoanalysis (Parts One and Two): Jesus As The Anti-Oedipus."[11] Vitz contends that Jung, Freud, etc., were correct in their descriptions of human behavior, but that Jesus is the answer because "Jesus is the anti-Oedipus." In the book *The Christian Vision: Man in Society*, Vitz says:

> And in the long run I believe it will be possible to "baptize" large portions of secular psychology; that is, to use what is valid in them, while removing their anti-Christian threat.[12]

If one reads Vitz's articles "Christianity and Psychoanalysis" (Parts One and Two) and the chapter in the above book, he will inescapably discover that Vitz is an integrationist. Because Powlison's integrationist view is a reflection of Vitz's integrationist view, Powlison may have been strongly influenced by Vitz.

Recycling and Reframing

The inner workings of the heart analysis (**inner counseling approach**), as practiced by Powlison and others, is the opposite of behaviorism (**outer counseling approach**), as practiced by Adams and others. We now reveal our concerns with the general teachings of that approach. Powlison provides a case study of Wally to exemplify this approach in an article titled "Idols of the Heart and 'Vanity Fair.'"[13] Powlison's article not only sets forth his expertise at "recycling" psychological counseling theories and therapies, but also reveals the fulfillment of his desire for CCEF to be "the ones who successfully will 'integrate' secular psychology," as stated years earlier in one of his articles in *The Journal of Pastoral Practice*:

> One of the ironies (whether it is bitter, humorous or sublime I am unsure!) attending the contemporary Christian counseling world is that **we, of all people, are the ones who successfully will "integrate" secular psychology.** "Integrationists" are too impressed with psychology's insights to be able to win them to Christ. Integrationists have missed the point that the big question between Christians and secular psychologists is not, "What can we learn from them?" The big question is, "How can we speak into their world to evangelize them?" But it is also fair to say that presuppositionalists have missed that the big question between biblical counseling and Christian integrationists is not, "How can we reject and avoid them?" The big question is, "How can we speak constructively into their world?"

> The key to both big questions is an ability to **re-frame everything that psychologists see and hold dear into biblical categories**. If we do our homework, then biblical counseling not only will be a message for the psychologized church. It will be a message for the psychologized world (bold added).[14]

Powlison saw problems with the way other people had been integrating psychology with the Bible. However, he fails to see that he is also too impressed with psychotherapeutic ideas, to the degree that **he uses psychological teachings and techniques that encourage believers to sin against one another**. His plan to "**reframe everything that psychologists see and hold dear into biblical categories**" has allowed him to simply organize and arrange those theories and techniques **that he believes to be useful** into a biblical framework. But, in doing so, the theories remain as deceptive as if they were in a secular framework. It is similar to the ways that people attempt to put evolutionism into a creationist framework. Either way, the Bible is compromised and people are deceived. Nevertheless, Powlison had dreams of winning those who didn't integrate biblically enough to his point of view:

> At minimum there are thousands of Christians, psychologists, psychiatrists, social workers, college psychology majors, counselees drinking from a different well **who can be won by an approach that interacts with and radically reframes what enamors them about psychology** (bold added).[15]

Here Powlison revealed his plan to appeal to other integrationists through reframing what "**enamors them about psychology**." But, **what enamors people about psychology is its appeal to the flesh!** Wouldn't Powlison thereby be appealing to a fleshly desire? In fact, should not love for and commitment to psychological theories and therapies be called an "idol of the heart"?

In his article "Idols of the Heart and 'Vanity Fair,'" Powlison reveals that he is continuing his quest to influence professional, psychologically trained Christians in the "helping professions." In the article he asks, "How do we legitimately and meaningfully connect the conceptual stock of the Bible and Christian tradition with the technical terminologies and **observational riches of the behavioral sciences**?" (p. 35, bold added). Throughout the article he shows how he connects idolatry, which he says is "the most frequently discussed problem in the Scriptures," to "the myriad significant factors that shape and **determine** human behavior," which are found in the psychological literature (p. 35, bold added).

"Recycling" or "reframing" are mere euphemisms for integration. **The idols-of-the-heart counseling is problem-centered "biblical" counseling psychologized.** Powlison and others at CCEF have made an idol out of idols-of-the- heart and have prostituted "biblical counseling" with the psychological problem-centered wisdom of men and ongoing sinful conversations. **Those at CCEF, while assiduously avoiding pietism, have become guilty of many psychologisms. In summary we say that, contrary to the claims and pretensions of CCEF, they are guilty of psychoheresy.**

Idols-of-the-Heart Counseling

Because Powlison's idols-of-the-heart, second-generation counseling is so well-known and used by many in biblical counseling circles, we critique it here prior to presenting his counseling case of Wally. Powlison argues that people develop idols of their hearts that usurp the love, devotion, trust, fear, service, attention, and delight that should go to God alone. Remembering that this is a metaphor, one could call anything an idol that usurps what belongs to God. However, in Scripture the references to idols generally have to do with actual idols, false gods, and false religions. In the New Testament the words translated *idol* refer to literal idols, false gods, or false religions.[16] Indeed, psychotherapy itself is a false religion.[17] Dr. Thomas Szasz aptly describes psychotherapy when he says, "It is not merely a religion that pretends to be a science, it is actually a fake religion that seeks to destroy true religion."[18] Nevertheless, Powlison finds the idol motif useful for incorporating elements of this false religion of psychotherapy.

In his attempt to recycle secular psychology, Powlison takes verses from the Bible about the world, the flesh, and the devil and says: "It is striking how these verses portray a confluence of the 'sociological,' the 'psychological,' and the 'demonological' perspectives on idolatrous motivation" (p. 35). He then uses primarily the psychological and sociological theories to discuss inward motivation and outside influences. He later admits, "My analysis has been psycho-social" (p. 47).

While some of what he says in this section is biblically sound, he nevertheless relies on the psychological theories to fill out the particulars of his model of counseling. He says:

> That idolatries are both generated from within and insinuated from without has provocative implications for contemporary counseling questions. Of course, the Bible does not tackle our contemporary issues in psychological jargon or using our observational data. Yet, **for example, the Bible lacks the rich particulars of what psychologists today might describe as a "dysfunctional family or marital system"** only because it does not put those **particular pieces of human behavior** and mutual influence under the microscope. The "lack" is only in specific application (p. 36, bold added).

Powlison considers these to be important additions. He obviously regards some observational details and theoretical constructs, such as psychological "family systems," to be accurate, or why would he consider them important enough for filling in what the Bible appears to him to be lacking? However, we must always keep in mind that these details, which are so important to Powlison, have been **subjectively** observed, recorded, organized, and theorized by people with deceptive hearts who disagree with each other.

According to the *Concise Encyclopedia of Psychology*, "There are currently four major schools in family therapy: object relations theory, Bowen theory, structural family therapy, and communication theory."[19] Since these family systems are not alike and some of their underlying "particular pieces of human behavior" contradict one another, which ones would Powlison have a counselor use? One of them, Object Relations Theory, originated by Melanie Klein, tends to be very long term, is very Freudian, and concentrates on "unconscious denied projections."[20] The other three systems differ in their own ways from this approach and from each other. None of the family systems approaches has been shown to be superior to the others, and no one, including Powlison, has demonstrated that "particular pieces of human behavior" derived from family systems are of any use, except as fodder for his fanciful fossicking.

Powlison's retrofitting of both family systems and psychodynamic psychology into his system of idolatry opens the door to some very sinful ideas and practices. He says, "Idolatry is a problem both rooted deeply in the human heart and powerfully impinging on us from our social environment" (p. 38). He thus connects the metaphor "idols of the heart" with psychological and sociological influences that significantly influence behavior and that must therefore be mined from the depths of the heart through insight and analysis in a manner similar to insight psychology. Thus, to find, identify, and deal with these idols of the heart, the counselor must find out lots of details about the counselee's family relationships. Such will require extensive understanding about these things from psychology so that a person will know what kinds of relationships might influence the individual to form various kinds of so-called idols of the heart. In fact, Powlison's approach depends upon finding the psychological underpinnings of behavior and figuring out which idols of the heart he might decide they are. The idols-of-the-heart system appears to fit nicely with the use of the unconscious in psychotherapy, especially since there are so many possible hidden idols to look for, identify, and describe.

Powlison finds it necessary to explore lots of details of "particular pieces of human behavior" in the psychological literature regarding such things as the "classic alcoholic husband and the rescuing wife" who "are enslaved within an idol system whose components complement each other all too well" (p. 37). While he recognizes that psychology is inadequate regarding "the interface between responsible behavior, a shaping social milieu, and a heart which is both self-deceived and life-determining" (p. 38), he wrongly regards various teachings from psychology as helping biblical counselors understand the complexities of the inner person. He says:

> Humanistic psychologies see the interplay of inner desire/need with external fulfillment or frustration.... Ego psychologies see the twisted conflict between heart's desire and well-internalized social contingencies (p. 38).

Why do Christians even need to know that kind of information? If one follows Powlison's logic and use of psychology, one could conclude that the Christians of the past, prior to the rise of psychological counseling after WWII, were handicapped because they did not have these latter day psychological "revelations."

Powlison says that "the behavioral sciences ... are idolatrously motivated" and "build into their charter and methodology a blindness to the essential nature of their subject" (p. 39). So, how can he trust what he calls the "rich particulars" (p. 36) from any of the psychological counseling literature? And, who decides which of the almost 500 conflicting approaches and which of the thousands of contradictory techniques have "rich particulars"?

Some years back we conducted a survey of the Christian Association for Psychological Studies (CAPS). CAPS members are psychologists of various kinds, many of whom practice psychotherapy and are committed to the integrationist view. We found in the CAPS survey how eclectic and, at the same time, different from one another these CAPS members were. Psychoanalytic, behavioristic, humanistic, and transpersonal psychologies were all possibilities for CAPS members. **As a result of our survey of CAPS members, as well as information from numerous other psychologists, we state categorically that all of these psychologists (every one of them) would no doubt claim to use "sound psychological principles" and would say they are completely biblical or at least do not violate Scripture, even though they use a variety of the many available psychological approaches, many of which contradict one another.**

Who is right and which one of these psychologized individuals should one believe and follow, including Powlison? As we describe and confront Powlison's recycled and reframed psychology, remember that all Christian psychologists are as completely certain, as he is, that they are truly biblical with their similar "recycling" and "reframing" psychology to "agree with the Bible." The difference is that Powlison appears to be confident enough to infer that he has it right; whereas all these other Christian psychologists have it wrong.

One is reminded of the Scripture of the blind leading the blind (Matt. 15:14). Even if Powlison picks and chooses according to the Bible itself, rather than imposing them into so-called biblical categories, his very picking may simply follow the idols of his own heart. There is really no end to guessing what idols of the heart may be hidden in one another's heart with so many possibilities and nuances that may come to mind, especially when one is well acquainted with the psychological wisdom of men.

Emphasizing the value of these psychological ideas detracts from his use of the Bible in his overall understanding. He says:

> Human motivation is … not strictly either psychodynamic or sociological or biological or any combination of these. These terms are at best metaphors for components in a unitary phenomenon which is essentially religious or covenantal. Motivation is always God-relational (p. 39).

Why doesn't he just stick with the final sentence from that quote, since the rest is unnecessary, superfluous, and downright distracting? One wonders why he needs all of these psychological ideas to supplement Scripture, since they cloud and distort the clear meaning of Scripture along the way.

Moreover, Powlison's system reduces all kinds of things to idols of the heart, which must be searched out and decided upon. Not only must these idols be found, but their source also must be determined. Although we can agree with Powlison regarding his statements that are biblically accurate, **we are opposed to problem-centered counseling conversations that come from seeking the source of the roots of behavior in ways similar to psychodynamic therapy as one can falsely**

biblicize them. In searching for the details to determine the specific idols in operation, much information must be unbiblically gleaned from a counselee, as will be seen in his case study of "Wally."

Problem-Centered Counseling with Idols for Every Problem

While Powlison and others at CCEF are in the business of searching for the idols of the heart, they are nevertheless problem-centered. His sixteen-page article begins with six-plus pages teaching about the idols of the heart and presenting the theoretical construct of his unbiblical problem-centered recycling approach to counseling as conducted by the CCEF idols-of-the-heart counselors. Next, the case of Wally reveals that the counselor works to unveil the heart and unravel the layers so that he can see what idols might be there, determine how they got there, decide how they function, and then transform the hidden motivations of the counselee into idols of the heart. The entire analysis is problem-centered and psychologically dependent. It is clear that Powlison had to spend lots of time conversing about Wally's problems in order to speculate about what's going on inside and attempt to fix the problems from the inside out. **In other words, the counselor, whose own heart is "deceitful and desperately wicked," must see into another person's "deceitful and desperately wicked heart" to deal with the problems of living, in spite of the Lord Himself declaring that He is the One who searches the heart (Jeremiah 17:9).**

Powlison seems to turn almost everything into idolatry. He says: "Idolatry becomes a concept with which to comprehend the intricacies of both individual motivation and social conditioning. The idols of the heart lead us to defect from God in many ways" (p. 37). Turning almost everything into idolatry is a convenient way for him to imbed the psychological counseling concepts he likes into his form of "biblical counseling." He justifies this by saying that "behavioral sins are always portrayed in the Bible as 'motivated' or 'ruled' by a 'god' or 'gods.'" However, he fails to support this "always" statement with Scripture. There are many instances in the Bible in which it was simply lust or sinful desire that motivated sinful actions. For instance, what god or gods motivated David to commit adultery with Bathsheba? There is no hint in Scripture that this was a god, unless, of course, David was his own god, but then one could understand every sinful motivation as due to idolatry of the self. And, if one does that, then one does not have to develop or learn an entire pantheon of idols, as in Powlison's idols-of-the-heart system. It really all boils down to God's way or my way, but if we do that, we have no justification for bringing in the psychological wisdom of men

What the Bible Says about Idols of the Heart

The word *heart* often signifies the inner man in Scripture and the word *idols* may be used metaphorically even though idols appear to be literal throughout Scripture. **However, there is no biblical basis for searching for idols of the heart as done by Powlison.** The phrase "idols of the heart" is absent from the major translations of the Bible. However, Powlison refers to Ezekiel 14:1-8 in his attempt to support his use of "idols of the heart." Ezekiel was a prophet of God and therefore received direct revelation from God: "Son of man, these men have set up their idols in their heart" (v. 3). When the men set up idols **IN** their heart, the idols were placed in the center of their devotion. There is a great difference between the two prepositions *IN* and *OF*. The word *OF* indicates belonging to, proceeding from, being a component, connection, or possession. Thus, the expression "idols **OF** the heart" indicates belonging to the heart, being an aspect of the heart itself, proceeding forth from the heart. The men setting up "idols **IN** their heart" in Ezekiel means that they have put them there, figuratively speaking, because of their heartfelt devotion to literal idols.

Ezekiel was not analyzing the men psychologically to gain insight into their heart to determine why they were doing what they were doing. Therefore Powlison's use of Ezekiel 14 to support his psychologically analytical scheme removes the context and distorts the meaning. In the context of Ezekiel 14:1-8, a comparison is being made between the men's outward worship of Jehovah and their real love and worship of the idols. The contrast is between their outward, insincere worship and inner, true devotion. Regarding Ezekiel 14:3, Matthew Poole (1624-1679) described these men as "resolved idolaters, their hearts were totally addicted to their idolatrous worship and ceremonies."[21] Because of the rampant idolatry at the time, those "idols in their heart" would have been related to actual idols, false religions, and false gods of the surrounding nations for which they had a heartfelt devotion.

To support his use of "idols of the heart," Powlison claims that 1 John 5:21, "Little children, keep yourselves from idols," must refer metaphorically to "idols of the heart" if the Scripture is to apply over time. However, the apostle John did not expand the meaning of idols and every reader at the time would have known he was referring to literal idols and false religions, because that was what many of them had left behind and could yet be tempted to worship. Turning these idols into metaphors to keep the Bible relevant to all periods of time is totally unnecessary since images, icons, statues, stones, and other physical forms of idols continue to this day and will continue until the return of Christ. Nevertheless, as mentioned earlier, the word *idols* can be used in a metaphorical sense. However, the Bible does not teach that there are idols in the heart that must be searched out by another human being through a psychologically contaminated system of insight and analysis. The Bible provides precise words regarding the source of sinful attitudes, thoughts, and motives, such as the word *flesh* used metaphorically throughout the New Testament in contrast to the word *Spirit*. Moreover, God has given every believer the Holy Spirit and the Word to enable each one to choose to follow the flesh or the Spirit.

Even if one is to use *idols of the heart* metaphorically, the Bible does not direct believers to search out one another's heart. Instead, the Lord does this. However, this latter-day psychological wisdom of men has given Powlison and his colleagues the notion that, by analyzing a counselee through extensive, expensive ($95 per hour) conversations focused on the counselee and his problems, they can know the idols of the counselee's heart.

Even the idea of believers searching for idols of their own hearts is absent from Scripture. The Holy Spirit is the indwelling counselor and is faithful to convict believers of their sinful actions, attitudes, and motivations. While believers are to examine themselves, the examination has to do with whether they are walking according to the Spirit by grace through faith. For instance, 2 Corinthians says, "Examine yourselves, whether ye be in the faith; prove your own selves. Know ye not your own selves, how that Jesus Christ is in you, except ye be reprobates?" The point of the verse has to do with the new life in them. Are they living by the new life Christ purchased for them or by their old fleshly ways? This kind of examination places more attention on the person of Christ than on the self. It's a reminder for believers to remember who they are in Christ. When they turn to Him they are enabled to walk according to the Spirit rather than the flesh. Hunting for idols, figuring out how they interact with other people's idols, and trying to get rid of them gives too much attention to the self, just like secular psychology. **The focus in psychology is the self; the focus in Christianity is Jesus Christ. Believers are to be "looking unto Jesus, the author and finisher of our faith" (Hebrews 12:2).** In fact, it is by looking unto Jesus that believers are transformed into His image: "But we all, with open face beholding as in a glass the glory of the Lord, are changed into the same image from glory to glory, even as by the Spirit of the Lord" (2 Cor. 3:18).

"Case Study and Analysis"

The actual dialogue and methodology of questioning, responding, and teaching are absent from Powlison's article. It is simply an analysis of poor Wally according to the so-called idols of his heart, how they developed, how he is "abused" by them (p. 42), and how they interact with the idols of the people in his environment. Powlison begins his case study and analysis by saying that he is "using a case study of a hurt-angry-fearful person" named Wally (p. 41). Powlison admits, "The external details of this case study are fabricated" (p. 41). We must add that, if they are fabricated, so are Wally's idols (inner details), as well as the account of how this kind of counseling helped Wally (p. 43). Nonetheless, **the case study does reveal how problem-centered, sin-saturated, and self-centered the idols-of-the-heart counseling is.**

Powlison begins by describing Wally:

> Wally is a 33-year-old man. He has been married to Ellen for eight years. They have two children. He is a highly committed Christian. He works for his church half time as an administrator and building overseer and half time in a diaconal ministry of mercy among inner city poor. He and his wife sought counseling after an explosion in their often-simmering marriage. He became enraged and beat her up. Then he ran away, threatening never to come back. He reappeared three days later, full of guilt, remorse, and a global sense of failure (p. 41).

Powlison describes Wally's "longstanding problems" as "anger, inability to deeply reconcile, threats of violence alternating with threats of suicide, depression, workaholism alternating with escapism, a pattern of moderate drinking when under stress, generally poor communication, use of pornography, and loneliness" (p. 41).

Violations of Scripture

Problem-centered counseling by its very nature is loaded with sinful communication and thereby often violates the very Word of God that biblical counselors claim to follow. We reveal a few of the many violations of Scripture in this section.

The following is said of Wally's father:

> Wally's father was a critical man, impossible to please. "If I got all A's with one B, it was 'What's this?' If I mowed and raked the lawn, it was 'You missed a spot behind the garage'" (p. 41).

Throughout the counseling it is very clear that Wally dishonors his parents and is encouraged to do so, thereby violating Ephesians 6:2-3. Otherwise there would not be so many negative statements about his father. However, such sinful talk is part of the process of problem-centered counseling and especially when the counselor is looking for psychological determinants of behavior in the unconscious. Powlison denies that he is doing that; however he is very close to it. He says:

> These forces and shaping influences neither determine nor excuse our sins. **But they do nurture, channel, and exacerbate our sinfulness in particular directions.** They are often atmospheric, invisible, **unconscious influences** (p. 44, bold added).

Wally describes his mother as "well-meaning, nice, but ineffective, totally intimidated by my Dad" (p. 41). Here he is dishonoring his mother, thereby again violating Ephesians 6:2-3. There appears to be no concern about such sinful talk during this kind of counseling. In fact, problem-centered, idols-of-the-heart counseling depends on this kind of information or misinformation. After all, this is only from Wally's perspective. One really hears nothing positive about his poor mother throughout the entire case study. Did she feed and clothe him as he was growing up? Did she take care of him when he was sick? Did Wally have one ounce of gratitude for his parents? No need to mention those kinds of things in problem-centered counseling. After all, the counselor is seeking out problems, with the counselee fixated on himself and his problems.

Wally describes his wife, Ellen, this way: "bossiness, nagging, controlling me, not supporting me or listening to me" (p. 41). Whether Ellen had anything to say in the matter is not clear, since this appears to be individual counseling with Wally, even though they both sought counseling. Powlison describes these people as if he knows them personally, when he really only knows Wally's parents through what Wally says, which is secondhand and obviously biased (Prov. 18:13, 17). Is that the way to know anybody? Moreover, he draws all kinds of conclusions about them and how they have influenced Wally with only Wally's say-so in an environment that leads to bad-mouthing the very people Wally is to honor. Much is said about Wally's father, mother, and wife and also about Wally himself. We are less concerned about what Wally says about himself, but very concerned about his sinful descriptions of his parents and his wife.

As in most problem-centered counseling case studies, Powlison utilizes the problems in Wally's life to demonstrate his model and methodology and to convince the reader of the effectiveness of this kind of counseling.

However, Powlison's insights are built upon a structure of biblical violations in what Wally communicates and, very importantly, on the fact that it is doubtful, as in most counseling, that Wally's descriptions are entirely accurate and trustworthy. As one becomes experienced in counseling, one learns that if the parents and the wives of the Wallys in counseling were asked to comment about how they are described, a different picture would emerge, invalidating both what the Wallys have said and what the problem-centered counselors have concluded through inferences, intuitions, and insights along with speculations and guesses.

Besides the serious violations of Scripture, one of the biggest drawbacks of problem-centered counseling is the untrustworthiness of what is said and heard and also of what is unsaid and unheard. For instance, throughout an entire year of counseling, the counselor may never even guess that a counselee has been sexually unfaithful during this entire time unbeknownst to the counselor and the spouse. Lots of talking with much analytical discussion and speculation often misses the real problem.

Because of the untrustworthiness of what counselees say, Wally's descriptions of his "critical" father and "ineffective" mother should be regarded as gossip (Proverbs 18:8). Wally's accusations of his wife "nagging and controlling" are a violation of Ephesians 5. Wally's description of the past week with an element of blame (p. 41) is unbiblical (Phil. 3:13-14). Wally presents himself as a victim and Powlison agrees (p. 42). And, most obvious, as we said earlier, Wally has dishonored his father and mother (Exodus 20:12 and Eph. 6:1-2).

Powlison does not divert Wally from his sinful talebearing, discrediting of his wife, blaming the past, playing the victim, and dishonoring his parents. Instead, Powlison participates in these sins and even amplifies them. He says:

> We see the dominion of a father whose leadership style was that of a tyrant-king, not that of a servant-king promoting the well-being of his son. In essence, he lied, bullied, enslaved, and condemned (p. 42).

Notice how Powlison, like the par excellence problem-centered counselor he is, believes Wally and says, "Wally's father was a critical man, impossible to please" (p. 41). Powlison represents Wally's father as saying, "You must please *me* in whatever way I determine" (italics in original, p. 42). Powlison later refers to "Wally's demanding and unpleasable father" (p. 45). Considering that no one can hear from Wally's deceased father, these are extreme accusations. **They demonstrate Powlison's penchant for believing and transmitting gossip and his creative writing abilities more than the truth.** All of this is part and parcel of problem-centered psychodynamic therapy.

Powlison buys into the psychological victimhood idea. **He describes Wally as a victim of his parents, of his wife, of the circumstances of his childhood, and even of his idols.** Powlison says:

> Wally was **conditioned** to be very concerned with what significant people thought of him. At the same time Wally bought the idol. He is simultaneously a **victim** and guilty. He was abused by powerful idols operative within his **family sys-**

> **tem**. He also instinctively both bought into those idols and produced his own competitive idols (p. 42, bold added).

Powlison also says, "Wally is psychologically controlled by a lush variety of false gods" (p. 44). Once counselors start down the "psychological side" and the "sociological side," as Powlison does, these sides become primrose paths on which one can trot out every possible creatively concocted interpretation limited only by one's imagination.

Helping Wally see himself as needy, emotionally wounded, and having been harmed, negatively influenced, or disappointed by others softens the biblical reality of responsibility, sin, and guilt, where the only true remedy is the cross of Christ and ongoing dependence on Christ for inner change and spiritual growth. Softening responsibility, sin, and guilt with all kinds of explanations of what happened in the formation of the inner person and how the inner person currently functions provides a different remedy (explaining and fixing the flesh) and ongoing dependence on the counselor, at least until Wally can identify and control the idols that Powlison points out. All in all, much of this sounds like a very fleshly pursuit. In fact, this kind of counseling would work just as well with professing Christians who are not truly born again.

The more Wally sees himself as a victim, the further he will move away from a recognition of his own depravity, the necessity of the cross, and love for the Lord, for His saving grace and for the new life He has given. The more he sees himself as a victim, the less gratitude he will have for his parents, his wife, and the Lord Jesus

Christ. **While there are true victims, focusing on their victimhood does not strengthen them anywhere but in the flesh.**

In his book titled *A Nation of Victims: The Decay of the American Character*, Charles Sykes says:

> The triumph of the therapeutic mentality … insisted upon seeing the immemorial questions of human life as problems that required solutions. The therapeutic culture provided both in abundance: The therapists transformed age-old human dilemmas into psychological problems and claimed that **they (and they alone) had the treatment** (bold added).[22]

Similarly Powlison sees the complexities of the inner life as problems that require solutions. Here we have a psycho-spiritual therapeutic mentality, where the idols-of-the-heart counselors are the experts and where "**they (and they alone) [have] the treatment**."

Powlison begins his section on "Multiple Idols" by saying, "We become infested with idols," almost as if they are external things like germs or pests (p. 43). If we are infested, is it really all our fault or is it that we really should not have left the honey on the counter to attract the ants or is it that we have neglected to call the exterminator? We know from Scripture that sin indwells all humans and that the "old man" is described as "corrupt according to the deceitful lusts" (Eph. 4:22). These are inordinate desires that indwell the inner person. Jesus did not die to save us from the influences in our lives or from some sort of infestation from without; He came to save us from our sinful condition and sins committed. Furthermore, **Jesus gave believers new life, not an idols-of-the-heart extermination manual.**

One Up / One Down

Powlison's statement, "We become infested with idols" has the pronoun "we." That is important because Powlison's possible "one-up" idols have a difficult time dealing with Wally's idolatrous mixture of desire for approval and resistance to being in the "one-down" position." Powlison says:

> The idolatrous patterns in Wally's relationship with his father manifest in other relationships. Wally has had ongoing problems with authority figures in school, the military, work, and the church.... Naturally, he brings this same pattern into the counseling relationship, with all the challenges that creates for building trust and a working relationship. He continues to manifest a typical stew of associated problems: a slavish desire to be approved, a deep suspicion that he won't be approved, a stubborn independency (p. 43).

Poor Wally! Even without being supposedly "infested with idols," the one-up/one-down counseling relationship alone can create that kind of mix, especially for men. Nevertheless, the counselor, being in the one-up position and having to engender trust, must exert his superiority, and this he will be able to do if he has a system with shibboleths known primarily to him. Because of the kind of counseling he does, Powlison cannot afford to meet on an equal basis at the foot of the cross in mutual care. After all, CCEF does charge money for one-up counseling or why else the fee?

Besides believing that he can discern idols of the heart in other people, Powlison makes the following claim: "Biblical counsel, **the mind of Christ about Wally's life**, can be given" (p. 43, bold added). The structure of that last sentence has "the mind of Christ about Wally's life" in the position of an appositive after the words "biblical counsel." An appositive is a grammatical form that gives an alternative meaning or further meaning to the noun preceding it. Thus in essence and in the context it is given, Powlison is claiming that, through his idols-of-the-heart system, biblical counsel can be given that is, in essence, "the mind of Christ about Wally's life." In fact, he says:

> As we have indicated, Wally's mass of behaviors, attitudes, cognitions, value judgments, emotions, influences, *et al.* can be understood right down to the details utilizing the biblical notion of idolatry (p. 46).

What a claim! What Powlison has actually done is simply categorize all these things and rename them as idols. In other words, he understands where everything fits into his preconceived grid. And this is "the mind of Christ about Wally's life"?!?

The pay-for-services power structure is very clear with the counselor in the one-up position supposedly giving Wally in the one-down position "the mind of Christ" about his life. **Scripture tells believers that they have the mind of Christ (2 Cor. 2:16); it does NOT say we have the mind of Christ for someone else.** The entire structure of the counseling is one-up/one-down with the counselor analyzing Wally and describing him in a very demeaning manner. Here are a few examples of how Powlison describes Wally:

> He oscillates between "flame-thrower and the deep freeze." On the one hand he can be abrasive, manipulative, angry, and unforgiving. On the other hand he withdraws, feels hurt, anxious, guilty, and afraid of people (p. 41).
>
> Wally continues to play out a three-fold theme. First, he typically rebels against certain dominant "successful people" cultures. Second, he finds his validity in the affirmation of a "down-and-out" subculture. Third, all the while he acts in idiosyncratic pride to create his own culture-of-one in which he plays king, and his opinions on anything from the dinner to eschatology are self-evident truth (p. 43).
>
> Certain gentle-faced idols—the mass media, professional sports, and the alcohol industry—woo him with temporary compensations and false, escapist saviors from the pressures generated by his slavery to the harsh, terrifying idols which enslave and whip him along at other times: "I must perform. I must prove myself" (p. 43).

Anyone who reads this article who intends to be counseled with this form of counseling should be prepared to be viewed, analyzed, and described psychologically in similarly demeaning ways. Just as we wonder how Wally's parents and wife would respond to his descriptions of them, we wonder how Wally would respond to such demeaning descriptions of himself in this "expert/dummy" relationship where the one who does the naming is the one who has the position of power, from which he claims to see into and analyze Wally's heart.

Methodology

Nowhere in the article does Powlison explain how he enables Wally to get rid of his vast infestation of idols or how to control them when they come into contact with other people's idols. Evidently the methodology is centered on the analysis of Wally according to the idols of the heart and then relating this so-called wisdom to Wally. Powlison says: "Wisdom, the nourishing and honeyed tongue, can make satisfying and convicting sense of things, and Wally can learn to live, think, and act with such wisdom" (p. 43). In other words after much conversation Powlison can, with his "honeyed tongue," sweetly point out Wally's many sins in terms of idols so that Wally can do the work of improving himself. That is exactly what most psychological counseling ends up being—self help according to whatever theoretical structure has been conveyed through the many expensive hours of counseling.

Therefore all that is necessary is to analyze Wally according to the idols of the heart, reveal those idols to Wally, teach Wally about how they motivate him, and possibly suggest tactics to disarm them—not that they are actually there, but that Powlison has said so. With this knowledge Wally may actually feel better about himself, in that he was not fully responsible for the formation of these powerful "idols" (p. 42ff). Maybe the idea is that if Wally can feel better about himself, he'll be willing to work on these idols that Powlison names. He may also feel empowered because he knows the names of the idols and understands how Powlison thinks they operate in his life. He may also be willing to follow along because now he's learning how to gain personal power himself by becoming a namer of idols, much like people gain a false sense of power in naming the temperament types of other people. After all there is power in being the one who names or at least knows the names. Wally may thereby become more self-confident with this information and even be able to control those "idols" to some degree by the power of the flesh, which doesn't mind as long as it is in control.

Powlison claims to know enough about what goes on in Wally's "complex heart and complex world to minister helpfully to him" (p. 43). Powlison does not even have to know all these things about Wally, let alone analyze them and talk-talk-talk about them at an hourly fee rate. God gave the method of communication: preach the Gospel and teach about sanctification. This is what was done in the early days of the church where people truly knew that they were new creatures in Christ.

The Bible does not give any indication that believers need to know anyone's "complex heart and complex world to minister helpfully to him." **In fact, a believer does not even need to know the sins, sinful motivations, or what Powlison identifies as the idols of the heart of another believer in order to effectively minister the life of Christ and encourage sanctification.** If believers need to know a fellow believer's "complex heart and complex world to minister helpfully to him," there would be clear instructions about this in the New Testament. Powlison's fascination and confidence in the psychological wisdom of men have corrupted his model.

In actuality all he has is external manifestations of the inner person from which he must assume, surmise, guess, and fabricate according to the system he has contributed to developing. That's really all the Puritan pastors had as they sought to search out the idols of the heart in their parishioners. In their attempt to help people, they also diverted away from full dependence on Scripture here, and, in doing so, prepared Christians to become more interested in finding out about the inner man. A book with the subtitle *From Salvation to Self-Realization* traces this history and reveals that the Puritan investigation into the inner man with the metaphor "idols of the heart" set the stage for the current-day acceptance and eagerness for counseling psychology.[23]

The "idols-of-the-heart" methodology cannot really bring accurate knowledge regarding the condition of the heart. It is limited to external indications of what might fit into one's preconceived pantheon of idols. After observing Wally's actions and listening to what he says about himself, the idols-of-the-heart counselor fits his own subjective observations into his idolatrous system. It's really all guesswork. **Powlison claims that Wally does not know what is going on inside his own heart, and, if truth be known, neither does Powlison.** However, with a system that groups certain actions, words, responses, and emotional expressions under various categories of idols, one could easily do that for oneself and others—and be completely wrong.

Yes, there will be some connection in some of the more obvious ones, especially those tendencies that most people have, such as one of their favorites, which is "fear of man." Such feelings are common to mankind.

Because many of the idols they have named have to do with various feelings and sinful attitudes and actions, counselees will very possibly admit to various idols that represent even fleeting feelings and temptations. In fact, some counselees will be more vulnerable than others to becoming overwhelmed with a whole host of idols assigned to them during counseling. Indeed, this reminds us of the title of Dr. Tana Dineen's book *Manufacturing Victims: What the Psychology Industry is Doing to People*.[24] A parallel might be something like Manufacturing Idols: What the Idols-of-the-Heart Counseling Industry is Doing to Christians.

After Wally learns all about his idols and the idols of those in his environment, he will still have quite a time keeping track of all of them and remembering which idol is interacting with which idols of the people around him. How can he even give attention to the Lord Jesus when he has to be watching out for all the supposed idols of his heart and those of people in his environment? It sounds like an arduous self-centered requirement. Moreover, he might easily be blind-sided by some so-called idols of which he is yet unaware. Then what? How much easier to follow the Bible and live by the new life Christ has given wherein Christ gets all the credit and glory rather than the person who is paid for dealing with everyone else's idols in addition to his own. More will be said about this shortly in "Wally and Christ-Centered Ministry."

This type of counseling is a very deceptive practice because people are led to believe that some people (i.e., "experts") can see right through them. Worse than that, they will think they now know their own inner idols and motivations and be further deceived. Then, if they don't feel or do better after all the counseling, they will assume that there must be more idols lurking in the wings and run back to the counselor who can supposedly see inside them. They may become thoroughly dependent on the expensive counselor to name the idols supposedly hidden in the heart, which in this kind of counseling seems to resemble a Freudian-type of powerful unconscious that drives behavior.

An Idolatrous System

Idols-of-the-heart biblical counseling is truly an idolatrous system. Just as the Israelites copied the nations around them and adopted their idols, so also have those who developed and use the idols-of-the-heart system been attracted to the psychological counseling systems of the world around them and then adopted aspects of those systems. As Powlison correctly says:

> With good reason both Old and New Testaments abound with warnings against participating in pagan cultures and associating with idolaters, fools, false teachers, angry people, and the like. Our enemies not only hurt us, they also tempt us to be like them. False voices are not figments which the individual soul hallucinates. "World" compliments "flesh" to constitute monolithic evil: the manufacture of idols instead of worship of the true God (p. 44).

Yet, that is exactly what recycling is. It is "participating in pagan cultures." Even Christians who have a strong grasp of Scripture seem to be easily tempted and drawn into the scientific-sounding academia of psychological theories and therapies. Indeed the world of psychological counseling compliments the flesh "to constitute monolithic evil: the manufacture of idols instead of worship of the true God." Here the hierarchy of idols includes such individuals as Sigmund Freud, Carl Jung, Alfred Adler, Abraham Maslow, Carl Rogers, and many others, primarily from the psychoanalytic, behavioristic, humanistic, and family systems branches of psychotherapy. Even though Powlison is really talking about idols of the heart, he actually gives a good description of the idols of psychology when he says:

> Such false gods create false laws, false definitions of success and failure, of value and stigma. Idols promise blessing and warn of curses for those who succeed or fail against the law (p. 42).

That is really an excellent evaluation of the fountains from which Powlison recycles and reframes to form his problem-centered idols-of-the-heart system. Indeed, he must have some love for those systems. Else why would he think it necessary to imbibe, recycle, and reframe from those various idolatrous systems and seek to fit them into "biblical categories"?

This polluted cistern of problem-centered, psychological counseling from which Powlison and other problem-centered integrationists have been drawing is loaded with the rottenness of evil, sinful speaking. Those who engage in problem-centered counseling, no matter what their positive motives may be, are often engendering strife in families as people talk behind one another's backs and say all manner of evil about them, whether true or false. When people speak evil of others, they actually increase their own negative feelings towards them to justify having said bad things. When people focus on how bad things are, they fail to see what is good. Rather than nurturing gratitude, these counselors may be nourishing ingratitude towards God and others. Rather than nurturing love for God and others, they may be feeding self-love and pride. Evil speaking of others is not edifying to believers (Eph. 4:29, 31). Therefore counseling that depends on it is sinful and will fail to nurture spiritual growth.

Powlison has turned his psychologically tainted system into a necessity for all Christians who would minister to fellow believers, for he says: "If we would help people have eyes and ears for God, we must know well which alternative gods clamor for their attention" (p. 44). However, the old self is the primary false god for everyone and that is why the flesh must be put off and denied. Self is the very essence of the psychological systems that have a host of things to look for in the self and a myriad of systems that must be learned and followed. If a believer were to have "eyes and ears for God," which seems like a rather pompous description for anyone these days, they would certainly not need Powlison's system of idols, no matter how those idols seem to fit the various manifestations of the flesh. If one is to have "eyes and ears for God" one must be much in His Word and in His presence. One does not have to memorize the names of an ever-expanding hierarchy of idols.

Turning "inordinate, life-ruling desires," and "human lust, craving, yearning, and greed demand" into idols removes them one step away from the person himself. An idol is not simply a sinful tendency of the flesh; it is still external to the person. It's not Wally; it's his idols that are the problem. They may be manifestations of his flesh, but they are not the totality of his flesh, which must be denied and put off. Wally's primary problem is that he is living according to what the Bible calls the "old man" rather than by the new life Christ purchased for every believer. This focus on idols does not disable or disarm the flesh, even though one may learn to rearrange the power structure of the so-called idols. In doing so, Wally might succeed in overcoming some of his anger, rebellion, fear, and sexual lust by strengthening his self-confidence and pride, even while believing he is becoming a truly humble servant.

Powlison says, "It is a curious but not uncommon phenomenon that a biblically literate person like Wally has no effective grasp on the idols of his own heart and the temptations of the particular Vanity Fair which surrounds him" (p. 47). Even a biblically literate person would have to learn the idols-of-the-heart system because they are not named as idols in the Bible. In this kind of counseling, one has to learn the system. Wally must have been aware of his own sins and sinfulness and of the sins of those around him. Otherwise he could not have communicated them to Powlison. Wally just had never thought of turning them all into idols that he could manipulate and manage. But now he has a way to look at his own life without becoming overwhelmed with the utter sinfulness of his flesh and without having to own up to the fact that he is evidently trying to live the Christian life through the power of the flesh.

We also wonder how biblically literate Wally is regarding the teachings about the new life in Christ and what sanctification is really all about. He seems to have been involved in a great deal of self-effort that did not succeed, and now he has embarked on a new path of self-effort where he has to keep track of all his idols and the idols of those around him. Wally needs to get back into the Bible itself and find his freedom in Christ.

Powlison says he has focused on "the issue of diagnosis" because "biblical diagnosis bridges immediately into biblical treatment" (p. 48). However, his analysis and treatment are not truly biblical. They are an amalgamation of psychological theories and therapies and the Bible, all wrapped together with four words, "idols of the heart," eisegeted to fit his commitment to recycling (integration). Believers do not need such a complex, convoluted psychologically contaminated system to discern whether they are walking according to the flesh or the Spirit.

The Flesh or the Spirit?

Powlison appears to consider his idols-of-the-heart counseling to be a means of sanctification. He speaks of salvation and then says, "But the ongoing work of renewal must engage him [Wally] genuinely over the particular patterns of idolatry that functionally substitute for faith in Christ" (p. 44). But, does an analysis of the flesh really enable a person to walk according to the Spirit? Prior to the current psychological era and prior to Powlison's idols-of-the-heart counseling there was a simple, understandable message: the Gospel, including the good news of Christ indwelling the believer through the Holy Spirit, and God's means of sanctification. No help was needed from the psychological wisdom of men. Paul speaks of salvation and the sanctification process following salvation in Colossians as a mystery that has been revealed to believers:

> Even the mystery which hath been hid from ages and from generations, but now is made manifest to his saints: To whom God would make known what is the riches of the glory of this mystery among the Gentiles; which is Christ in you, the hope of glory: Whom we preach, warning every man, and teaching every man in all wisdom; that we may present every man perfect in Christ Jesus (Col. 1:26-28).

Powlison describes Wally as a Christian who "loves Jesus Christ" and "believes the Gospel" and "desires to share Christ with others" (p. 42). If he is indeed a Christian, why should Wally wallow in his sinful flesh searching for idols when he has been enabled to walk according to His new life in Christ? Perhaps because the clear Bible message has been clouded by Powlison and confused with the worldly psychological methods of self-improvement.

The "old man" is indeed a complex mixture of the evil effects of the world, the flesh, and the devil, but we do not need to analyze it, because it cannot be repaired. It had to be replaced. **Sanctification has nothing to do with analyzing and fixing the old man or the flesh. It has to do with walking according to the new life in Christ.** Nevertheless Powlison offers as a method of sanctification his "*process* of inner renewal" (p. 50, italics in original). Next he says, "Jesus says to take up our cross *daily*, dying to the false gods we fabricate, and learning to walk in fellowship with Him who is full of grace to help us" (p. 50, italics in original). Jesus is speaking of more than "false gods we fabricate." Jesus is speaking about our entire old selves. There was no way to save ourselves through any system. Christ, in dying in our place, took our sinful lives with Him and gave us new ones. Indeed, we are to **daily** take up our cross and reckon our old man crucified on the cross with Christ so that we say can with Paul, "I am crucified with Christ: nevertheless I live; yet not I, but Christ liveth in me: and the life which I now live in the flesh I live by the faith of the Son of God, who loved me, and gave himself for me" (Gal. 2:20).

Why focus on Wally's problems that relate to his sinful flesh? Why turn all of this into a host of idols? Such a counseling approach will draw counselees into the flesh rather than into the Spirit. It appeals to the flesh, because the counselee is front and center, explained, and even exonerated to some degree. But believers are not to walk or even change according to the flesh. Why not break the pattern there instead of using psychological pieces of information to detect and dissect the very thing that should be put off (Eph. 4:22)?

Because Powlison's system of sanctification relies so heavily on the wisdom of men about which the Bible warns (1 Cor. 2), it could easily end up being a religion of works whereby one climbs up the ladder of self-improvement, thereby empowering the flesh rather than encouraging true spiritual growth. After undergoing idols-of-the-heart counseling, will Wally truly love the Lord Jesus more? Or, will he become more confident in his management of the idols? Will he become more dependent on Christ or on this new self-knowledge? Will he be growing spiritually or simply strengthening his flesh?

Will he become more Christ-centered or self-centered with this new-found self-knowledge that requires so much ongoing attention?

Idols-of-the Heart Conclusion

Recycling, reframing, categorizing, and searching for the "particular pieces of human behavior" in psychology do not make any of the secular, fleshly origins and practices of counseling psychology biblical. Powlison may not see that he truly is an integrationist just like all the rest of them, even though his approach is beautifully crafted and categorized in such a way that, when one reads his descriptions of biblical counseling, one may easily be deceived into thinking that what he is advocating is truly biblical. Particularly in his section on "What is the Gospel?" it is clear that Powlison desires to bring forth spiritual growth through identifying and dealing with the idols of the heart. Nevertheless, when he describes the content of the counseling, one sees that his reframing and what he calls "recycling" end up being filled with fleshly activities and much sinful speaking.

Counseling that comes forth from such astute psychological integration will tend to strengthen the flesh rather than nurture the new life in Christ. One may admire Powlison's ability to recycle, reframe, categorize, and describe his system, because he has indeed reached a veritable pinnacle of integration. However, we wonder if his integration might be more dangerous than some of the other forms, simply because his is so beautifully crafted with Scripture and influential argumentation. Yes, his integration might indeed be superior to all others, but then hasn't every Christian integrationist thought he was combining the best from both worlds in the best possible way? **Above and beyond all of this idols-of-the-heart counseling mess is the important fact that Powlison's problem-centeredness involves speaking evil about others and is therefore sinful to the core and should be avoided by all believers.**

Wally in Christ-Centered Ministry

We will consider just a few things to think about regarding how a fellow believer might assist Wally through Christ-centered ministry. In Christ-centered ministry the person who ministers **would not have to know details about Wally's past or even much about his problems**, since they would not be the focus of ministry. There would be no need to analyze Wally to figure out what makes him do what he does and feel what he feels, since Scripture is very clear about the difference between walking according to the Spirit and walking according to the flesh. The focus would be on Christ and the Word of God in reference to Wally. The ministry would be mutual care in the sense that both believers meet at the foot of the cross on equal ground where Christ can minister truth and life to both of them. While there would be teaching and reminding, the one who ministers would endeavor to avoid the pitfalls of one-up/one-down counseling and would certainly never charge a fee for ministering to a fellow believer.

The goal would be for Wally to come to know Jesus Christ more fully as Lord and Savior and as the lover of his soul in the nitty-gritty of daily living. Therefore the person who ministers would strive to nurture Wally's love relationship with Christ and to **help him see how**

problems of living can be used for spiritual growth. The person who ministers would attempt to guide the conversation towards the ongoing work of Christ in Wally and away from sinful kinds of conversations that are intrinsic to problem-centered counseling as practiced in idols-of-the-heart counseling.

When people like Wally are experiencing the kinds of problems described by Powlison, they need to see their problems from God's perspective. Here problems of living can serve as a wake-up call to walk according to the Spirit rather than the flesh. Therefore the discussion with Wally would involve how the Lord has already worked in his life. Wally would be asked to talk about those times when he turned to Christ and found Him faithful. Wally could relate instances when he experienced confidence in Christ's life in him. We would also want to know about his understanding of the Gospel, his own depravity, the great love of God, the wonder of Christ's death in his place, and the life of Christ indwelling him through the Holy Spirit.

The Bible teaches believers that they have been given new life: "Therefore if any man be in Christ, he is a new creature: old things are passed away; behold, all things are become new" (2 Cor. 5:17). Therefore, **instead of having to learn about all the details of how Wally's "old man" functions according to the deceitful lusts, we would give attention to how the new man in Christ functions in Wally**. Then Wally will learn to notice whether he is following the sinful ways of the "old man" or the new life in Christ. He will even be able to learn to pick up on early clues of reverting to the flesh before suddenly finding himself expressing more gross aspects of his sinful flesh. The Bible clearly details the differences between the flesh and the Spirit in Galatians 5 and says, "Walk in the Spirit, and ye shall not fulfil the lust of the flesh.... And they that are Christ's have crucified the flesh with the affections and lusts. If we live in the Spirit, let us also walk in the Spirit" (Gal. 5: 16, 24-25).

Rather than learning the idols-of-the-heart system, Wally needs to give more attention to the kind of fruit he is producing. In other words, certain sinful feelings, such as hateful, bitter, envious, or prideful feelings, can serve as a signals that he is walking according to his old life and that he needs to immediately turn to the Lord and repent before he allows his flesh to take him any further into sin. Believers need to practice nipping the old flesh in the bud before it blossoms forth into further sinful talk and actions. If Wally is truly a believer, he has the God-given responsibility and ability to choose to walk according to the Spirit moment by moment. **This is active faith, not any kind of passive piety**. God has given the new life in Christ and thereby the power to choose His way instead of the sinful ways of the old self.

We would talk about what it means to walk by faith, as Colossians 2:6 says, "As ye have therefore received Christ Jesus the Lord, so walk ye in Him." Wally needs to have a clear understanding of the new life he has been given and to learn to walk according to that new life. As a matter of fact, Wally may know all of these doctrines even better than the person who is ministering to him. He may just need to be encouraged to apply what he knows.

Then for those times when Wally reverts to his old sinful patterns, we would want to encourage him to continue to turn to Christ, no matter what. In that way he will learn to see that whenever he reverts to any of his old sinful ways of thinking and acting he is walking according to the flesh rather than the Spirit. We would want to talk with him about all Christ has done for him and remind him that at any point of difficulty he can turn to Christ and walk according to the Spirit. This can be done instantly (often if necessary) through moment-by-moment repentance. 1 John 1:9 reminds believers of the constant availability of shifting from the flesh to the Spirit: "If we confess our sins, he is faithful and just to forgive us our sins, and to cleanse us from all unrighteousness." For the Christian the most prevalent sin is going our own selfish, fleshly way instead of walking according to the new life Christ has given. The more Wally turns and chooses to walk according to the Spirit, the more he will recognize those times when he has reverted to the flesh and he will grow in his experience of walking according to the Spirit rather than by the old sinful ways of the flesh.

If Wally talks about his problems, we would ask him what the Lord might be teaching him and how he can apply the Scriptural admonition to be thankful in all circumstances (1 Thes. 5:18). Or, we might ask him how he might use various problem situations for spiritual growth. If Wally begins to complain about his parents or his wife, we would explain that such talk would not be helpful to him and could be harmful, because it may lead to dishonoring his parents and wife and to other forms of sinful thinking and talking. We would not want the ministry time to deteriorate into speaking evil about others. We would ask him to think of those people in a more merciful light and talk about what he can be grateful for regarding his parents and his wife. We might ask Wally to express his thanksgiving to God for the blessings he has received. Beneath all the sinful talk that Powlison described about Wally's parents, one can see that Wally's parents were probably fairly decent, hard-working, and conscientious. They obviously wanted the best for their son and it appears that his mother was submissive to his father. **Wally would be better off developing a grateful heart and a merciful manner than sinfully downgrading and dishonoring his parents and wife.**

As Wally finds more for which to be grateful he will see more ways God has blessed him and revealed His love for him. Even in the worst of circumstances, one can find things that reveal God's love behind the scenes, even if it is an expression of the Father's love in disciplining His child when necessary. Here it would be thanksgiving for the fact of belonging to God. At all times we would want to encourage Wally to see how much God loves him, because it is out of God's love for him that Wally will love God and others, which is the heart attitude of one who is walking according to the new life in Christ as a child of his heavenly Father.

Also, it is vital to remember the presence of the Lord in every situation, whether to comfort or correct or both, whether to encourage or admonish or both, but always to use every situation to conform Wally to the image of Christ and to bring him to maturity. Furthermore, Wally needs to know God in His fullness, rather than through a skewed perspective.

Because Christ-centered ministry is mutual care, those who minister to Wally need to recognize that they can learn from Wally as well as from the Lord during each occasion of providing ministry. Since Wally may indeed have a real heart for souls and for ministry, he needs to be treated as a fellow soldier in the warfare described in Ephesians 6:10-20. We would certainly remind him that he needs to be availing himself of the whole armor of God all the time, since he is on the front line of the battle for souls. **In the idols-of-the-heart counseling he is treated as though he is a victim of idols rather than a soldier equipped for battle.** If Wally is truly born again, Christ has prepared him for life, service, and warfare. Christ-centered ministry should then serve to strengthen him in the Lord and remind him of all he has in Christ to enable him to walk by faith and to "stand against the wiles of the devil," which can be especially fierce when Christians are about the Lord's business of proclaiming the Gospel and caring for the needy.

It is so easy for those who are in ministry to become so involved in ministry that they neglect their own personal time with the Lord in **daily devotions**, Bible reading, prayer, and worship. Just as we emphasize the importance for all believers to be **walking daily** with intentional times of Bible reading, prayer, and worship, we would doubly emphasize that importance for those in full-time ministry and for all believers when they are experiencing problems of living.

4

Dr. Heath Lambert

In addition to Dr. Jay Adams and Dr. David Powlison, Dr. Heath Lambert is one of the best-known, highly respected leaders of the biblical counseling movement in the world. Lambert's credits include the following:

> Dr. Heath Lambert is the Executive Director at the Association of Certified Biblical Counselors. ACBC is the largest biblical counseling organization in the world with counseling training centers and certified counselors in 29 countries. [1]

Lambert also serves as the Co-Pastor at First Baptist Church in Jacksonville, Florida, and is a faculty member at The Southern Baptist Theological Seminary.

In his popular book *The Biblical Counseling Movement After Adams*, Lambert describes his "Grand Unifying Theory" (GUT), which unites all "the idols of the heart" back to "a self-exalting heart that grasps after autonomy."[2] Thus, he takes what he considers to be helpful from Adams and from Powlison for his third generation of biblical counselors. The following two cases by Lambert reveal how he counsels and how biblically sinful biblical counselors can be. The second counseling case, in which the husband is a porn addict, is biblical counseling at its worst and is certainly a further demonstration of what's really sinful about even the best of biblical counseling.

"Sarah" and Postpartum Depression

Heath Lambert, coeditor of *Counseling the Hard Cases (CTHC)*, presents the case of "'Sarah' and Postpartum Depression." He admits in his first footnote:

> I have worked with several couples who had struggles similar to the story told here. This case study combines details of these different situations. None of the identifying information in this chapter matches that of the real persons involved.[3]

In other words, the case of Sarah is a reconstruction by Lambert from the stories of "several couples who had struggles similar to the story told here." "Several" means more than two. Were there three or more? Were all as successful as the contrived combination of several couples? Or did Lambert take the success of one and stir in the ingredients of all, including those cases in which he may have failed? How long ago did the several cases rolled into one take place, and what is similar about them? Remember that Clark and Sarah do not exist, but are figments of Lambert's imaginative reassembling of several cases resulting in a refined recapitulation.

We would label this case as doubly jeopardized with respect to reality. Real cases are literal cases with literal dialog. A reconstructed case is once removed from truth, but a **combination of several cases** into one is twice or thrice removed from the unvarnished truth!

To his credit, Lambert was not counseling Sarah alone, but included her husband, Clark. To his discredit, Lambert is guilty of personally usurping the husband's authority in the presence of his wife. But to his credit is Lambert's involvement of many in the church to support and assist Sarah and Clark. This is commendable and copyable for others to follow, provided that no mention is made of all of her symptoms, as this could legally jeopardize them, as we will explain shortly.

Lambert describes Clark and Sarah's background, including the birth of their baby and the dramatic aftereffects on Sarah. He also describes the extent of Sarah's symptoms that precipitated the need for help:

> Finally, on the afternoon that Clark had called me, Zoe had been crying as Sarah was beginning to prepare dinner. As Sarah held a knife, she began to plan a scenario of picking up Zoe, slamming her on the floor, and slitting her own wrists. At that point Sarah realized that she needed help (p. 88).

Lambert then follows with a section on "The Secular Diagnosis" (p. 90). In this section he delineates differences between "postpartum depression" (PPD) and "postpartum psychosis" (PP), which only occurs rarely. Lambert explains the usual treatment route that is followed in such cases and comments as follows:

> Interestingly, although most psychologists believe that hormonal shifts have something to do with PPD/PP experiences, such a view has never been documented. The only hormonal treatments are uncommon and experimental" (p. 91).

Lambert is establishing that there is not a medical problem or he would have said so and would not have written up a case of PPD/PP. To eliminate the possibility that hormones are involved, he makes claims about "hormonal shifts" and "hormonal treatments." To prove his claims, he gives a footnote with three references, the first and third of which contradict his claims.

For Lambert to say that the "hormonal shifts" view "has never been documented" is false. The dictionary says, "Something that is documented has been written down or recorded."[4] PPD/PP symptoms and treatments are well documented in the literature. Maybe Lambert meant "proven," but if he did he should have said so. His second claim that "The only hormonal treatments offered are uncommon and experimental" is also false. "Experimental"? Yes. "Uncommon"? No. The dictionary definition of "uncommon" is "unusual" or "rare." We did an internet search of "estrogen treatments for postpartum depression" and found that they are all "experimental," just as there are many other experimental attempts to deal with many other diseases, but there are too many of them to call them "uncommon." The following is from Lambert's first footnote reference (p. 91), which contradicts his view:

> Seven women with histories of puerperal psychosis and four with histories of puerperal major depression were consecutively treated with high-dose oral estrogen immediately following delivery.... This low rate of relapse, 9% compared to an expected 35-60% without prophylaxis, suggests that oral estrogen may stem the rapid rate of change in estrogen following delivery, thereby

> preventing the potential impact on dopaminergic and serotonergic neuroreceptors.[5]

In other words, hormone treatment has proven helpful.

Lambert's second reference supports his view, but is dated February 2003. However the third reference given by Lambert, dated October 2010, does not support his view (p. 91). The reference is to Thomas R. Insel, MD, when he was director of the National Institute of Mental Health. Insel speaks about "research to expand the understanding of the causes of, and treatments for, postpartum conditions" and says:

> What new treatments are on the horizon? In preliminary trials, 17-beta estradiol, a form of estrogen, was shown to have a relatively rapid antidepressant effect in women with PPD, faster than typical antidepressant medications like SSRIs, which can take up to 8 weeks to start working. And unlike antidepressants, evidence suggests that the increased levels of estrogen associated with the treatment are not detected in breast milk, and therefore presumably do not pass to the nursing newborn.[6]

After discussing two studies, Insel says, "Both of these studies provide evidence that the change in estrogen levels during the postpartum period may be a primary hormonal trigger for PPD."[7] Again, Lambert's reference does not support his teaching.

Lambert has bypassed the recent research and painted a simplistic picture for other biblical counselors to draw from and tragically counsel women with PPD/PP symptoms who may have biological issues behind their symptoms. One would think that Dan Wickert, MD (OB/GYN), who did one of the ten cases in *CTHC*, would have warned Lambert about PPD and PP. We can only guess that Wickert, an OB/GYN doctor, agrees with Lambert's conclusion about Sarah being a non-medical case.

Like other cases in *CTHC*, Lambert reconstructs with perfection on what he says and what he does during the counseling sessions with occasional self-compliments on pp. 86, 94, 98, 99, 103, and 110. This sounds bizarre to us, as Lambert took several stories, massaged them into one, gave retrospective words to the one manufactured case and lauds himself along the way.

Lambert says:

> I also insisted that Clark make an appointment for Sarah to see her physician as soon as possible. The Bible's clear teaching on the importance of the body encourages seeking the assistance of trained medical professionals in situations such as this (p. 97).

He also says, "In such instances a couple should demand that their medical providers administer physical exams and appropriate laboratory testing to rule out any organic causes for their problems" (p. 97). **However, no matter how much laboratory testing one does, that can never entirely "rule out any organic causes for their problems."** Serious errors result from this type of reasoning. First is the mistaken idea that one can know whether or not mental symptoms that are not clearly "caused by brain damage, tumors, gene inheritance, glandular or chemical disorders" are actually "nonmedical problems." Medical doctor Barbara Schildkrout, in her book *Masquerading Symptoms: Uncovering Physical Illnesses that Present as Psychological Symptoms*, lists 71 diseases that may cause mental, emotional, or behavioral symptoms that may precede other symptoms. She then describes mental, emotional, or behavioral symptoms as they may relate to each of the 71 diseases.[8]

The fallacious assumption that Lambert and others present in *CTHC* is that, unless there are proven biological diseases that can account for the usual symptoms of mental disorders, the root causes and cures are spiritual and can be resolved biblically. Lambert contends elsewhere: "Receiving a full medical work-up allows us to rule out organic issues."[9]

Since one cannot always know whether or not there are "organically generated difficulties," one should not conclude with Lambert that the mental disorders are spiritually driven, thereby only needing biblical remedies.[10] The truth is that in such complex cases as PPD and PP only God knows whether the symptoms are due to physical changes, emotional factors, lifestyle influences, spiritual issues, or a combination of all of these. Lambert has decided that Sarah's disorder is not due to physical changes. This is an error that many may copy to the detriment of the women involved.

Lambert reports that:

> Sarah did go to see her OB/GYN the next day; but unfortunately, the visit did not go well.... After asking her a few questions, her doctor insisted that Sarah seek psychiatric help. He informed her that he would check up on her in coming days, and if she had not contacted a counselor in the

> next day or so, he would be forced to report her to Child Protective Services. Thankfully, he was satisfied when they informed him that they were already meeting with a counselor, and they never heard from him again (p. 97).

Lambert gives his prior counseling experiences with similar situations and then says, "However, I say it to encourage women who are experiencing similar difficulties **to avoid merely reporting their situation to their physician**" (p. 97, bold added). This could be a seriously misunderstood bit of counsel. What is similar? Lambert should have warned other biblical counselors that every state has its own child abuse laws. Although in some states a pastor may have clergy protection under "penitential communication," non-pastors would no doubt be required to report all "similar situations" or be breaking the law for not doing so. Therefore, if those in the congregation were privy to all that was told to Lambert, they would be obligated by law to report it. Since Lambert is a quintessential biblical counselor and a distinguished leader in the biblical counseling movement, he is sure to be imitated and trusted. Many will read his advice to "encourage women who are experiencing similar difficulties to avoid merely reporting their situation to their physician" and advise the same under "similar circumstances," which may be to their own legal detriment, as they would be privy to information that would have to be reported.

As Sarah was recovering, Lambert says:

> It was now time to address another area where Clark and Sarah needed to encounter Christ.... I now needed to shift to another area— the ways in

> which Clark and Sarah had each sinned against God and against each other in their situation (p. 106).

Typical of the biblical counseling movement is the counselor taking it upon himself to confront the counselees' sins. Lambert says: "There were definitely specific areas where Sarah needed to pursue confession and repentance of sin. One area was her responses of sinful anger toward Clark and Zoe" (p. 107). He later speaks of Sarah beginning "the process of confessing her sin to God, to Clark, and even to [baby] Zoe (why not?)" (p. 108).

Lambert not only points out her sinful responses under duress, but informs her that she has had a pattern of anger since childhood and that her weakened condition was no excuse. Whoa! Wait a minute. Let us recapitulate. Lambert says:

> As a child she had a difficult relationship with her mother. They were never close. Her mom abused alcohol and had a terrible temper. Sarah observed her mother's fits of rage as she would yell and throw whatever was nearby. As Sarah grew up, she began to imitate her mother. Her life was marked by severe fights that would often result in yelling and throwing anything in sight. These incidents had subsided when Sarah became a believer. They vanished completely when she married Clark (p. 89).

Biblical counselors believe that they must find reasons for specific sinful behavior before they can help. Therefore they open the door for the counselees to sinfully dishonor parents (Eph. 6:2-3). For Lambert to describe Sarah's mother this way, Sarah herself had to have described her mother in a manner that was selective and personally biased (Prov. 11:13; 18:17, 26:22).

Why look for reasons for specific sins of the flesh when the answer is to put off the "old man" or flesh and put on the new life in Christ? Nevertheless Lambert, having explored Sarah's past, leads Sarah to believe that "she had never dealt with the patterns of anger she learned in childhood" and now needs to repent according to his prescribed manner. Lambert says:

> Sarah began to realize that she had never dealt with the patterns of anger she learned in childhood. Instead, they had just gone dormant. When she was living with her mother, Sarah's anger would constantly flare up. While living with Clark, her external circumstances had changed, and the temptation had abated. Now that her temptation had returned, the sinful disposition of her heart reared its ugly head and revealed her need to repent (p. 107).

Distinguished professor and memory expert Elizabeth Loftus says that in counseling, "just because someone tells you something with great detail and confidence and emotion, it doesn't mean it happened. So just being open to the possibility that you're dealing with the product of some process other than an authentic memory recovery would be a step in the right direction."[11]

Questions: How does Lambert know this description of Sarah's mother is accurate? Answer: He does not know for sure! A whole host of questions come up that Lambert cannot answer. For examples: would Sarah's mother agree that she "abused alcohol" or just drank occasionally? How often did Sarah's mother exhibit "fits of rage as she would yell and throw whatever was nearby"? Once? Twice? Regularly? We do not know and Lambert would not know either! Why does Lambert deal with the distant unknown past, which is completely unnecessary to know in order to minister to Sarah? This is more psychological than biblical.

The combined case of Clark and Sarah, admittedly assembled from similar stories of several couples, strikes us as a presumptuous unbiblical demonstration, as Lambert remonstrates against this couple. Lambert has mercilessly butted in and biblically battered both Sarah and Clark in his attempt to address their sins against each other and against God. He describes Sarah's sinfulness in some detail. According to Lambert, Jesus was bringing her to a realization of sins of pride and selfishness, but one wonders how much coaching she was getting from Lambert, who clearly confronts Clark with the following words: "You know, Clark, I wonder how you missed all of Sarah's struggling going on right under your nose?" Lambert then says, "This question cut Clark to the core." He then judges, "Clark was now realizing that his presumptuous behavior was recklessly selfish and unloving" (p. 108). In the process, Lambert pitilessly pours pious platitudes about his biblical right to do so, without properly parsing the Scriptures and absent of any connection between the various verses he quotes and the reasons he gives for why he should take the one-up position on this (p. 107).

The spiritual headship of men is easily corrupted in problem-centered counseling and the place of the wife is also corrupted by Lambert (1 Cor. 11:3; Eph. 5:22-33). Lambert has unbiblically usurped Clark's biblically rightful place in his relationship with his wife and takes authority away from Clark. In doing so, he in essence becomes Sarah's spiritual head (like a surrogate husband) as he leads her in confession and repentance of sins committed within the confines of marriage with seemingly little sympathy for her weakened condition.

Rather than Lambert unbiblically and unmercifully violating Clark's spiritual authority, thus obscuring Sarah's biblical relationship to her husband, which is sinful in itself, it would be better to encourage them into a daily walk with the Lord and to trust the Holy Spirit to convict them of past and present sins. There is something terribly demeaning to have the counselor engineer the whole process rather than allowing the Holy Spirit to do what He does best. When a counselor confronts any sin that a person has committed against anyone but himself, choreographs what is to be said and done, and then oversees the operation, there is a greater possibility for superficiality than true genuine confession, repentance, and forgiveness. During such times, as experienced by this aggregate couple going through the trials, tribulations, and sufferings of life, those who minister must remember the biblical possibilities of encouraging them into a daily walk with the Lord as a means of drawing them close to Him. The Lord can do much better than a human counselor in confronting them with their sins, which is the work of the Holy Spirit.

A Failed Biblical Counseling Case

The Institute for Biblical Counseling & Discipleship (IBCD) has a Core & Discipleship Certification (CDC) Program, which is "designed to help churches develop one another care in the life of the congregation." One can be certified by IBCD, and "The CDC process also brings one along towards the ACBC [Association of Certified Biblical Counselors] Certification if further certification is desired."[12] The IBCD offers the IBCD Observation 12-Disc Set and also a 3-disc observation set by Dr. Heath Lambert counseling "Jeremy" & "Crystal," titled "Counseling Care for Pornography." We elsewhere critiqued the prior 12-disc set[13] and now review the 3-disc set.

The following announcement precedes the beginning of the three recorded sessions of counseling:

> The following observational sessions are fictional but based on real life scenarios. The participants did not have a script but are reacting and improvising in much the way they would in a real life setting.

True, the participants did not have a word for word script, but the counseling was structured in advance and playacted predictably to a successful conclusion.

Jeremy & Crystal

The accompanying booklet describes the counseling case as follows:

> These three videos focus on Jeremy, a church-going, hardworking husband and father of four, whose long-standing enslavement to pornography is tearing his family apart. His wife Crystal

> is threatening to move out following a recent incident in which their daughter walked in while her father was viewing inappropriate material on his computer. Jeremy has come for counseling as a last ditch effort to save their marriage.

Additionally, we learn that Jeremy, who is 37, first looked at porn when he was 9 and 10 and then regularly watched porn since he was 15. He admits that he has been watching porn for 22 years.

Joseph J. Plaud, a private, clinical, forensic psychologist who has studied the effects of pornography, warns about how the need for more stimulation increases the more a person watches porn. He says, "The more you do [it] and the greater degree of access, the more explicit [it is], you seem to need more and more."[14] Jeremy admits to watching movies of porn that are visual, active, and auditory. Thus, we conclude that Jeremy has been viewing hardcore pornography for most of his life.

Jeremy's 11-year-old daughter caught him not only watching porn movies, but Jeremy confesses, "I was covered up, but I was doing what guys do when they look at porn." Jeremy's wife, Crystal, who is pregnant with their fourth child and is expecting soon, has threatened to move out unless Jeremy's problem "gets fixed." The first counseling is with Jeremy alone; the second and third recorded counseling sessions are with Jeremy and Crystal.

Lambert shows compassion and portrays the issues and problems with some appropriate biblical references in Part I. However, although Lambert recognized that Jeremy had a questionable testimony as to his salvation, there was no real effort to find out Jeremy's understanding of salvation. This is a serious omission on Lambert's part. Even though Lambert may have felt it necessary to go gingerly with Jeremy and not confront him directly, he could have asked questions about the necessity of the cross and his understanding of human depravity, the goodness of God, and the new life in Christ.

A survey conducted by LifeWay Research for Ligonier Ministries indicates:

> One of the most troubling findings in the survey is the lack of understanding Americans have regarding sin and the total depravity of human beings. Actually the majority of Americans perceive goodness to be a better description of people.... 67% agree "Everyone sins at least a little, but most people are by nature good."[15]

Lambert spent most of his time durng the first session in a teaching mode. Human depravity should have been uppermost, because this is where a person may get a glimpse of the depth of his own sinfulness and the vast magnitude of God's love. Considering Jeremy's superficial testimony and his 22-year relationship with hardcore pornography, Lambert should have probed this one serious doctrine or at least mentioned the importance of doing this in future sessions during his "Final Recap."

To his credit Lambert rightly assigned Ephesians 2:1-10 as homework with instructions to read and interact with this passage every day. However, there is no indication of any follow up by Lambert to see whether he pursued the content and intent of these verses with Jeremy regarding the depravity of man and the goodness of God. Later, when Lambert asked Jeremy about the high points of the preceding months of counseling, nothing was said about this Ephesians passage or this essential doctrine.

Although Jeremy admits that he had always felt dirty and that 1 John 1:9 was helpful, we wonder if he ever understood the depth of his own depravity, how much he had offended God, and the extent and great cost of forgiveness he had received. There seemed to be far more emphasis on fixing the problem than on honoring and glorifying God.

The counseling in Part 2 with Jeremy and Crystal deteriorates as Lambert usurps the biblically required authority and responsibility of the husband (Jeremy) by choreographing the words for Jeremy to say to Crystal. As we said regarding Lambert counseling Sarah and Clark, we repeat here: There is something terribly demeaning to have the counselor engineer the whole process rather than allowing the Holy Spirit to do what He does best. When a counselor confronts any sin that a person has committed against anyone but himself, choreographs what is to be said and done, and then oversees the operation, there is a greater possibility for superficiality than sincere genuine confession and repentance.

Also, we have shown, both biblically and practically in our critique of *CTHC*, why a man should not be counseling a woman, as Lambert does and has done, even if her husband is present.[16] It would have been far more biblical and effective if Lambert had counseled Jeremy alone and had a woman minister to Crystal. This will become very transparent as we review Lambert's third recorded counseling session.

Egregious Errors

The counseling continues and, at the beginning of Part 3, Lambert says, "Well I cannot believe how far we have come in just a few months actually." To convey to other biblical counselors that in "just a few months" Lambert succeeded in transforming a 22-year hardcore pornography user, who is doubtfully a Christian and who has had slips during the "few months" of Lambert's counseling, into a recovered case is an egregious error that should not have been playacted for others to believe and follow.

The most practical part of Part 3 is Lambert suggesting that Jeremy have a post-natal plan to serve Crystal and being specific about what can be done instead of focusing on his own sexual desires. This third playacted session then deals with the subject of Crystal's upcoming post-birth condition, which was said to make her unavailable for sexual intercourse for six weeks, and the impact that may have on Jeremy's perceived dire necessity for sex possibly precipitating a return to pornography. Lambert says, "As far as sexual intimacy is concerned, why don't you look at Song of Solomon, Chapter 2." Lambert then reads verses 3-7 from the *English Standard Version* (*ESV*):

> As an apple tree among the trees of the forest, so is my beloved among the young men.
>
> With great delight I sat in his shadow, and his fruit was sweet to my taste.
>
> He brought me to the banqueting house, and his banner over me was love.

> Sustain me with raisins; refresh me with apples, for I am sick with love.
>
> His left hand is under my head, and his right hand embraces me!
>
> I adjure you, O daughters of Jerusalem, by the gazelles or the does of the field, that you not stir up or awaken love until it pleases.

After reading the Song of Solomon, Lambert explains:

> What the woman is saying here is that—using very poetic imagery—she's saying that in their intimate relationship there was an entire banquet of things that they were doing together. And she is saying, "I enjoyed all of them. I enjoy being with my husband sexually in **all the ways** that you can be." So I think this is a passage of the Bible that teaches us poetically that there's **all kinds of things** that married couples can do to enjoy one another in the context of sexual intimacy (bold added).

Lambert later says:

> This is a picture of a woman who is **loving the buffet of sexuality** with her husband and, in the context of that, she delights to be embraced by him (bold added).

The meaning of **"all the ways"** as in "I enjoy being with my husband sexually in all the ways that you can be" is "in every way." The meaning of **"all kinds of things,"** as in "there's all kinds of things that married couples can do to enjoy one another in the context of sexual intimacy," is "an unlimited number of things." The word *buffet*, as in **"loving the buffet of sexuality"** means a tempting variety of sexuality. **In no way is it possible to infer or imagine that the woman in Song of Solomon would be interested in or expecting pornographically inspired sex, but Lambert fails to explain this to Jeremy and Crystal!** This is a serious omission as Lambert euphemistically describes the possibilities: "You don't have to have sexual intercourse in order to be able to be sexually fulfilled during this season of your marriage."

A little later Lambert explains:

> And so, this can be a time that is really sweet for both of you. She's going to be—she's going to have some limitations on her physical body as to **how she can serve you in that way—but she can still serve you**. But you ["Jeremy"] are going to be **unlimited** in your ability to draw near to her to embrace her, to rub her arm, to rub her hair until she falls asleep (bold added).

The word *unlimited*, as in "But you [Jeremy] are going to be unlimited," simply means that there will be no limit to Jeremy's "ability to draw near to her."

Alhough all of the above seems well-intentioned, it is ill advised and is an egregious error and sets an unbiblical example for counselors to follow, which any hardcore porn user can capitalize on. Jeremy confessed in Part 1, "I don't ever ask her to like **act out** the porn scenes or whatever. I would never ask her **to do** that" (bold added). But he then says, "There are things I would like for us **to do**, but she's just not—I guess—as willing **to do**" (bold added). Now Lambert opens the door for Jeremy to have "unlimited" kinds of non-vaginal sexual activity with Crystal.

While Crystal may hear tender loving care, such as embraces and having her hair rubbed, Jeremy is no doubt hearing permission to act out and experience the kind of pornographic sex acts he has looked at and pleasured himself with on the internet. Because of his heavily promiscuous (22 years) participation while watching pornographic acts and his "slip-ups" during the few months of counseling, Jeremy needed restraint! But, Lambert gave none!

Two other egregious errors to note: First, there is an innuendo in this playacted scenario that puts the burden on Crystal to serve her husband or else he may resort to pornography. Second, Jeremy, through over 12 years of marriage, has had sexual intercourse with Crystal and at the same time used hardcore pornography to pleasure himself. It is an egregious error on Lambert's part not to know that Jeremy will likely do the same during the six weeks after the birth of their fourth child, where he has been promised **unlimited** sexual possibilities with Crystal.

More Egregious Errors

Lambert again usurps the husband's (Jeremy's) God-given role and becomes a surrogate husband to Crystal. He asks Crystal:

> Would you feel comfortable being with him sexually and even satisfying him in a way that did not include the kind of sexual activity that you can't have because of your physical condition?

In response to Lambert's leading question, Crystal naively agrees. This is another egregious error on Lambert's part.

Lambert is familiar with postpartum depression (PPD) and postpartum psychosis (PP),[17] which can occur after giving birth to a baby. Mayo Clinic describes both:

> Many new moms experience the "postpartum baby blues" after childbirth, which commonly include mood swings, crying spells, anxiety and difficulty sleeping. Baby blues typically begin within the first two to three days after delivery, and may last for up to two weeks.
>
> But some new moms experience a more severe, long-lasting form of depression known as postpartum depression. Rarely, an extreme mood disorder called postpartum psychosis also may develop after childbirth.
>
> Postpartum depression isn't a character flaw or a weakness. Sometimes it's simply a complication of giving birth.[18]

In fact, some PPD can last up to 2 and 3 years.[19] Also some mothers experience breastfeeding pain.[20] All of the above could dramatically affect Crystal's availability for sexual intimacy for some time! And yet Lambert in no way brings up the very facts of which he is well aware to alert Crystal and Jeremy of these possibilities. Crystal not only has limitations on her physical body as to how she can serve Jeremy, but she may have other postpartum occurrences that should have been explained by Lambert, but tragically were not!

Lambert has glossed over Crystal's post-birth needs, which are to be sacrificed on the unbiblical altar of pleasing Jeremy's sexual desires as a possible protection against his pursuing pornography. Lambert's counseling is a prime example of why we recommend against men counseling women, as this reveals how severely sympathetic Lambert is to Jeremy's sexual "needs" and how seemingly unsympathetic he is about Crystal's possible postpartum condition when he opens Pandora's box of euphemized sexual possibilities in reference to her serving Jeremy.

From all the material we have read and the various Christian pornography-recovery websites we visited and called, we conclude that this a deviously deceptive and seductive playacted case that should not be believed or followed. In his book. *Finally Free*, Lambert says, "For the past decade, I have spent thousands of hours talking with hundreds of people who struggle with pornography."[21] **Based on his many years of experience and many individuals struggling with pornography, Lambert should have known better and certainly should have done better!**

Conclusion

Lambert is one of the major leaders in the biblical counseling movement. He is sure to be trusted, trumpeted, followed, and imitated. All three recorded sessions were predictable because the elements were surely structured and playacted toward a successful conclusion. However, they should not be taken literally as a prescription or plan to follow in counseling men who are enslaved to porn; i.e., Lambert's playacted case should not be re-enacted by counselors with their counselees. **Lambert's unbiblical example of marital counseling and his extremely egregious errors should not be emulated. This is a failed counseling case for Dr. Heath Lambert, which**

once more proves our contention that the practices of present-day biblical counseling reveal the unbiblical errors of the movement. The various examples of the unbiblical practices of the leaders in the biblical counseling movement, such as Lambert, should discourage all Christians from signing up for any of the certificate/degree programs.

We repeat from our past writings: The biblical counseling movement is a recent phenomenon in church history. **The certificate/degree training programs are entirely unnecessary for believers to minister effectively to fellow believers**. These were not necessary before the latter-day appearance of the biblical counseling movement and they are totally unnecessary now. The certificate/degree-oriented biblical counseling organizations act as intimidators and disablers of mature believers who would, with a little encouragement, minister to fellow believers in need. This smacks of a one-up/one-down relationship where the one-ups should step down.

From our many years of experience, we know that there are numerous Christians who are mature in the faith who would be blessed to minister to others in the fellowship, but who do not do so because they feel blockbustered by degree or certificate granting, one-up training organizations and educational institutions that promote training followed by more training. While we are opposed to Christians enrolling in any certificate or degree biblical counseling program to learn such systems and methods of counseling, **we do encourage those who wish to minister to others to increase their Bible knowledge, to attend Bible classes, or to enroll in a**

biblical studies degree program rather than a biblical counseling degree program.

5

Dr. John Street

Dr. John Street is a professor of biblical counseling at The Master's University and Seminary (TMU&S). He previously served as a pastor for 22 years and also taught at Cedarville University and Cornerstone University.[1] Street's teaching and counseling reveal the influence of the three generations of biblical counselors found in the Association of Certified Biblical Counselors (ACBC), formerly titled National Association of Nouthetic Counselors (NANC), and the Biblical Counseling Foundation (BCF). As such, he leads the graduate program in biblical counseling at TMU&S.

Over five years ago we wrote a three-part article series titled "A Critical Review of the Master's College & Seminary Biblical Counseling Program," in which we show Street's unbiblical counseling practices. **The following is a modified version of Part One and Part Three** with some adjustments having to do with the names of biblical counseling movement associations and the upgrade of The Master's College to University:

A Critical Review of The Master's University & Seminary Biblical Counseling Program

Part One

The Master's University & Seminary is touted as "one of the leading schools for undergraduate and graduate level training in biblical counseling." In fact, The Master's University and Seminary (TMU&S) conducted a survey of "all the Christian counseling programs that are accredited graduate level throughout the United States" and found that, as far as could be determined from the research, TMU&S "had the largest graduate program in the country." They also reported that, whereas "the average Christian counseling accredited graduate programs has about 40 to 50 students in it," TMU&S has 270 students.[2] In addition to having a very large biblical counseling program, TMU&S, with its association with Grace Community Church, wields a tremendous influence in the biblical counseling movement (BCM) nationally and internationally, especially because of the leadership of Dr. John MacArthur. **Because of its popularity and great world-wide influence, we will be answering this critical question: Is the highly touted, popular, and widely influential biblical counseling program at The Master's University and Seminary truly biblical?**

In this series of articles we will demonstrate that the head of the biblical counseling program at TMU&S models the use of sinful speaking, eisegetes Scripture to justify his counseling, and teaches two egregious ideas. All of this is not only taught to the students at TMU&S, but also spread worldwide. We conclude the series with recommendations for correction. **To determine wheth-**

er or not the programs at TMU&S are biblical, it is necessary to put to the test primarily what they do and say during counseling, not just what they say about counseling. We all know the saying, "What you do speaks so loudly I can't hear what you say." We have often said that one must evaluate biblical counselors by what they **do** in the counseling room, rather than by what they hope to do based upon what they say and write.

In order to find out what they do, it is necessary to find actual live counseling sessions on video, audio, or print and compare what is seen and heard with the Bible. Compared to the plethora of counseling materials that merely talk about the various facets of counseling, there are very few that present literal live counseling. The ones we have examined demonstrate very clearly that the most popular approaches **are actually unbiblical**. This includes the approaches promoted by the National Association of Nouthetic Counselors (NANC) [recently changed to the Association of Certified Biblical Counselors (ACBC)], the Christian Counseling and Educational Foundation (CCEF), and the Biblical Counseling Foundation (BCF).[3]

We have said for years that the major error of the biblical counseling movement is that **they are problem-centered with sin-saturated conversations, just like the psychological counseling movement. We have proved repeatedly in our writings that problem-centered counseling inevitably leads to sinful communication.** Some time back, to expose this issue in the biblical counseling movement (BCM), we presented the following challenge:

> With the thousands of individuals claiming to do biblical counseling and the Bible colleges and seminaries that teach it, one should be able to find a biblical counseling session (or a series of sessions) in writing or on audio or video that is truly biblical and therefore having no sinful speaking. **We challenge biblical counselors to provide a word-for-word counseling session or a detailed description of one to demonstrate that they are truly biblical.**

To date no one in the BCM has answered that challenge.

Until recently we have had no literal counseling sessions to evaluate the counseling program at TMU&S. However, we found a web site that does have two audios, which include live biblical counseling sessions in addition to a number of lectures by biblical counselors **about** biblical counseling.[4] The actual counseling is conducted by Dr. John Street, who chairs the graduate program in Biblical Counseling (MABC) at TMU&S.[5] Obviously what Street does in his biblical counseling is what he teaches his students and what he promotes through his numerous contacts worldwide.

Street's Videos and Audios

We listened to all of Street's audios and videos available from the Biblical Counseling and Discipleship Association, So. Cal. (BCDASoCal), Fall 2011 Training Conference.[6] We also read the PDFs of his talks. Using Street's videos, audios, and PDFs, we will now evaluate what Street does in his biblical counseling and demonstrate that he, like other biblical counselors, is contrary to the Bible, because in the context of problem-centered counseling he expects and encourages responses that necessarily involve sinful speaking.

Joe and Julie

There are two audio sessions that include Street counseling Joe and Julie, a married couple.[7] We learned that there were three DVDs with parts of ten counseling sessions on them. We attempted to obtain the three DVDs but were prevented from doing so even by a web site that at first sold us the three DVDs, but then, prior to filling the order, returned our payment and removed the three DVDs from the site. Therefore, we were limited to the two audio sessions.

The couple that Street counseled used their first names and identified the husband, Joe, as being a pastor at Faith Community Church. We wanted to contact them for an interview, because, as reported in a professional journal, "Controlled outcome studies show that only about half of couples improve with treatment. And even among those who do make progress a disheartening chunk, 30 to 50 percent, relapse within two years."[8]

Therefore, we contacted Pastor Bruce Groves, Vice President of BCDASoCal, and after several email exchanges learned that the Joe and Julie counseling sessions were actually **re-enactments**, meaning that **these were not truly original live counseling , but re-enactments of what was supposed to have happened in the counseling sessions.** We asked Groves if the Joe and Julie in the ten counseling sessions were the original counselees. He said that the Joe and Julie in the recorded counseling sessions "**were re-enacting the counseling scenario of another couple**"[9] (bold added).

Think about it! The real Joe and Julie are not available for us to contact and confirm what happened; the Joe and Julie actors were apparently following a made-up script; the dialog leads to a fabulously successful tenth meeting conclusion; and **none of this is verifiable!** We suspect that this Joe and Julie scenario is tailored to a fabulous conclusion that might be discredited by the original Joe and Julie if we were to contact them. As we add up all the concerns we have about this wonderfully successful ten sessions of counseling by Street with the faux Joe and Julie, we conclude that there would likely be a great discrepancy between what originally happened and the acted out "re-enactment."

Next, let us look at the apparent success of the counseling sessions. We say "apparent" because, as we said, there is no way to follow up with Joe and Julie to see if the happy ending continued on or deteriorated after the final session. In other words, were the weeks and months after the counseling ended as successful as it seemed in the last session of the re-enacted counseling?

The outstandingly successful Joe and Julie counseling touted by Street could unfortunately be the very reason for the popularity and interest in the TMU&S biblical counseling major. However, our past research has revealed that counselors regularly use successful counseling stories to promote their approaches.[10] Providing playacted counseling sessions in biblical counseling not only shows people how to do it, but provides a platform to promote the methodology by showing how well that approach works. **Do not be intimidated** by such demonstrations of biblical counseling that appear to prove an approach or point of view of the biblical counselor or are used to demonstrate how to counsel, whether presented in writing or given verbally at conferences.

Observing demonstrations of counseling can actually get in the way of personally ministering to fellow believers. Two people could have exactly the same external problem, but only God knows the specifics of what and how for a particular person. This is why we say that those who minister to one another need to get **in** the way and **out of** the way. They need to be available, but they need to let God work rather than push their own agenda.

We have never seen a literal failed counseling approach revealed in all the biblical counseling writings we have examined. We have seen biblical counselors blame their counselees for failures or give examples of poor counseling on the part of others, but none that have displayed their own failures. Revealing only the successes gives the false impression that if you follow the method displayed, you too will find success.

The truth is that counselors and especially counselors with an agenda (their particular approach) too often take credit for successes and attribute failures to the counselees. The trumping truth is that success is primarily in the hands of the counselees,[11] and those who counsel must not take credit for success or use the success to promote their point of view as a result. **Otherwise, they are bound in fairness to take the blame for their failures and to reveal their methodology that failed.**

Counseling Session

As we asked at the beginning, "Is the biblical counseling program at TMU&S truly biblical?" It is not even how successful it may appear to be, but rather how biblical it is that counts. Street begins the counseling session in a manner quite similar to other nouthetic counselors when he says, "I want to be able to address **everything** that we can in order to be of help to you." (Bold added.) Street elsewhere refers to Proverbs 18:13: "He that answereth a matter before he heareth it, it is folly and shame unto him."[12] This verse sets the stage for Street to ask Joe and Julie personal questions and to encourage them to hold nothing back that may be helpful, thereby **pressing them beyond biblical limitations to sinful speaking**. Yet, in order to honestly and accurately hear the matter, all parties involved should really be heard and that includes those not present, such as spouses, parents, in-laws, other family members, friends, coworkers, etc. All counselors would need to hear from all the people their counselees talk about behind their backs to really know what's going on according to Proverbs 18:17: "He that is first in his own cause seemeth just; but his neighbour cometh and searcheth him."

What follows comes from some of the information gleaned from Joe and Julie each completing the Personal Data Inventory (PDI). The PDI requires one to list "Identification Data (Personal), "Health Information," and "Marriage and Family Information." At the end of the PDI are the following six questions:

1. What is the main problem, as you see it? (Why are you here?)

2. What have you done about it?

3. What can we do?

4.Describe your spouse's personality in a few words (selfish, loving, etc.)

5. As you see yourself, what kind of person are you? Describe yourself.

6. Is there any other information we should know?[13]

The use of the PDI amplifies the problem centeredness of the counseling because many more problems are brought up than necessary with more to talk about unnecessarily. The PDI also opens many doors to sinful, unbiblical speaking, which is amplified by putting such thoughts in writing.

Instead of counseling according to the PDI, which invites sinful communication, those who minister must bring the ones in need of help into a daily walk with God, in which they will seek Him in His Word, pray, and open themselves to the work of the Holy Spirit. Then, as they respond to God they will know what to do by trusting and obeying Him. As God does the inner work and they respond, the glory goes to God and not to man. Personal ministry must be done without sinful, unbiblical conversations that regularly occur through the use of the PDI and other means of digging deeply into the lives of those in need.

Many problem-centered counselors consider the PDI, which only recently arrived in the history of the church, and other such inventories to be valuable, but they are often a detriment when ministering biblically. The PDI is just one more look-alike from the psychological counseling movement. Also, using the PDI is entirely unnecessary as thousands of individuals who call themselves biblical counselors and others who minister biblically have never used one and could claim equally successful cases as the one presented by Street. Prior to the creation and use of the PDI Christians throughout the history of the church ministered to one another and they were in no way hampered or restricted by the absence of anything like the PDI. Actually the PDI with its possible long list of problems could focus on the flesh and divert the counseling away from what the person truly needs: a growing daily spiritual walk with God.

Biblical Standards of Communication

The bottom line is whether or not the words spoken by Street, Joe, and Julie meet biblical standards. **The counseling stands or falls on whether or not they meet biblical standards in practice.** Joe and Julie are members at Faith Community Church and Joe is a pastor there. Julie teaches school and is pregnant. They are in counseling because they are having marital problems.

In this counseling session Joe does most of the talking, which is unusual for most marital counseling.[14] Although Joe makes some self-effacing comments, he primarily complains about his wife, is highly critical of her, and exposes what he considers to be her faults to a third party. Such descriptions elicited in the biblical counseling environment are filled with violations of 1 Corinthians 13:4-7; Ephesians 5:22-33; and 1 Peter 3:7. The third party (counselor) is usually only an acquaintance or a stranger, who is both eliciting and listening to these sinful conversations, all of which are expected as part of the usual biblical counseling process.

As with most biblical counselors, Street encourages unbiblical remarks along the way. The following are **a few of the many questions** Street asks in the process of digging for problems and their details:

> Can you tell me a little more about that?
>
> Are there any other areas?
>
> Is there anything you want to add to that to help me understand it?
>
> So what else would you like to add to that?
>
> How are you dealing with that?

Street further advances openness and exposure of the couple by saying, "But what you're sharing with me is helpful." With Street's encouragement, support, and expectation, **Joe makes a number of clearly unkind, unbiblical remarks**.

Street asks Joe, "Can you tell me a little more about that? What do you mean by anxiety?" Joe's answers:

> I have expectations of her and **she seems to always fail** at meeting those expectations as far as being the pastor's wife that I think she should be in the local church where we're serving. We have wonderful opportunities for ladies ministries and whether it be calling on the phone or sending little notes of encouragement or sharing with the ladies in Bible studies—are things that—she's just not rising up to meet those expectations at all, or even the responsibilities that some of the

> other ladies think she should be involved in (bold added).

There is no cautioning Joe with such passages of Scripture as in Ephesians 5:22-33, James 5:20, and 1 Peter 3:7 about how he is to love his wife by not complaining about her or giving a bad impression of her to others. Instead, Street asks, "Are there any other areas that you believe are kind of a source of your anxiety?"

In response to Street, Joe continues to **spiritually slander his wife** by saying:

> Maybe some of my background growing up in a pastor's home I saw things one particular way as a pastor's wife should handle things and she doesn't live up to that right now and I want to get her there as fast as I can. And she's slow and hasn't had that same background and so part of it is just impatience I think.

After assuring Joe that they will work together on this problem, Street broaches another subject by saying, "Now, you also mark down here 'communication,'" and then asking, "What do you mean by communication? What's going on there?"

Joe explains and then says, "Her life is not participating in the life of the ministry in the church where I am." While Joe takes some of the blame, he nonetheless says of Julie:

> **She doesn't feel like I care or understand** about where she is in the home. And at the same time I feel like **she has no idea of what I'm experiencing in the church**. And so we communicate in different terms, and there's times where I just

> come home and don't even want to say anything to her **because she won't understand**. And she's thinking so much about the home front and her needs and I think **there's just a lot of selfishness there** and maybe even some blindness on my part of failing to understand the different trials and the different circumstances that are troubling her (bold added).

Street's marital counseling depends upon counselees speaking evil of one another in violation of Proverbs 11:13; Ephesians 4:15, 29; James 3:2-8; and Titus 3:2. Although counselors may believe that they are simply exposing what needs to be addressed, they are actually exacerbating problems through inviting and listening to such sinful communication.

Full Exposure Required

While Street makes a few brief remarks after each exposure, these problems are not addressed beyond asking for more details. The NANC [ACBC] process calls for every problem to be laid out on the table and described in as much detail as possible during the sessions. As Randy Patten, former executive director of NANC and reviewed here in Chapter 8, declares that it is necessary to "**understand completely** what is going on" before giving any advice so that the counselor won't be "a fool in God's eyes" or give "lousy advice" (bold added).[15]

Street then continues to probe into another subject. Evidently in reference to Joe's answers on the PDI, Street says, "You also talk about your physical relationship in marriage—**your sexual relationship**" (bold added). He then ventures into this highly sensitive area by asking, "And why did you mark that as part of the problem here?" Street is obviously fishing for details about their sex life. We cover this same subject in Chapter 8, in which Pastor Patten pursues a couple whose husband says, "I'm very dissatisfied with our sex life."[16] We mention this to show that such excursions into this sensitive and biblically sacred area of marriage by biblical counselors are not unusual. Street is only doing what is standard for many and what he teaches others to do.

As we say about such needless excursions: This reveals how deeply worldly this counseling is and the extent to which psychological problem-centered counseling with its expected transparency resulting in sinful communication has been emulated and embraced by the church. As much as prying for details is expected and practiced in biblical counseling, details about a couple's intimacy should not be shared with a third party in counseling. Nevertheless such problem-centered counseling depends on such details even in these intimate areas. However, there are ways to minister to couples without invading their bedrooms and physical intimacy through unnecessary sinful communication.

In response to Street's question about the lack of sexual intimacy, Joe describes his frustration, which includes the following words:

> Well, I think just a desire that obviously it's probably more apparent in the man versus a woman as far as for that sexual need to be met. Where there's that desire to be met even on a weekly basis at times, or a couple times a week.

Joe criticizes Julie, who is **pregnant and teaches school all day**, for not being available for sexual intimacy! He then says, "I want to enjoy her," and, "She's too tired to really enjoy any times like that." Joe "generously" confesses that he doesn't "have to have this all the time."! Then he uses the Bible to justify his complaint:

> It's a biblical desire that God has given to both of us to love to have, and we want to meet that in one another, but I think just the way our lives are going in two different directions, it's just hard to meet at that time to where this can happen on a consistent basis. And, because of that, I have a hard time getting to sleep. Sometimes we'll just go to bed and I can't get to sleep because I know I've been denied the satisfaction and she's just gone to sleep on me.

Joe then says that, as a result, "Anger sets in and just frustration at why she is unwilling to do this."

Street responds by affirming, "Okay, what you're saying is really helpful." Helpful? Perhaps as far as getting as much information as possible, which is the nouthetic method. However, the marriage bed is holy and for Joe to expose his wife in the way he does is sinful! This kind of talk in real counseling would surely make a woman feel she has been betrayed both by her husband and their counselor. This excursion by Street into the privacy of Joe and Julie's sexual intimacy is a reflection of worldly counseling rather than a biblical need.

While the topic of sex is clearly dealt with in Scripture, Paul was no doubt answering general questions in 1 Corinthians 7 rather than having private sessions with couples during which they expose one another! One does not need to hear the complaints or the details to teach about marriage. Biblical counselors would do well to skip the preliminaries (the digging and prying) and teach the doctrines and principles from Scripture, thereby **trusting the Holy Spirit to do the convicting and the inner work for outer obedience**.

The very fact that a couple would return for the next session after the counselor has usurped the spiritual headship of the husband and led him into betraying his wife shows how the ways of the world have deceived even those who think they are being biblical into making such a mockery of the biblical one-flesh principle (Eph. 5:31-33).

The next subject Joe brings up at the prompting of Street is "the importance of spending devotional time together." Joe says of Julie:

> She doesn't want to wake up in the morning. She doesn't want to give me that time. She would much rather have her own time in bed and she wakes up just—and even kind of angry as far as why I would want to insist this upon her this early. **So it's kind of like duplicitous of her to be saying that and then to not have any desire for that** when it's something that we like to develop in our lives (bold added).

As Street allows (even encourages) such talk, possibilities for bitterness can increase on the part of both Joe and Julie. Nevertheless, Street lets Joe continue to insult and demean his wife in his presence.

Then, because they are not spending prayer time together, Joe concludes that this lack has "affected her personal devotional life with the Lord" and accusingly complains:

> **...she talks to me like she has never even studied the Bible recently. Just the way she acts and behaves, there doesn't seem to be any connection there of Biblical truth and how she's living her life** (bold added).

What an insult! This is pure and simple sinful talk by a husband against the wife he is to spiritually nourish and support. This kind of talk will not serve to build a one-flesh relationship.

Joe reveals elsewhere that "within a couple years or so things have slowly started to digress." In describing their relationship Joe says, "There haven't seemed to be any real substantial change that has been continuous." With Street being an elder at Grace Community Church and with Joe already having had two years of marital troubles, one would think that, if Joe were a pastor there, John MacArthur would at least have called a time-out on his ministry, but Street says nothing about this.

A Few Simple Questions

We have commented on only the re-enacted part of one counseling session conducted by Street with Joe and Julie and used examples from Joe's remarks to reveal the extent of the unbiblical sinful speaking that occurs in his biblical counseling. **Imagine hearing all ten counseling sessions, greatly compounded with more sinful speaking, as encouraged by Street and followed by Joe and Julie.** Add to that the important fact that Street is training students at The Master's University and Seminary along with others world-wide in this sinful speaking, unbiblical approach offered as biblical help. They will surely desire to replicate what he does, especially with such a positive ten-session ending.

Now that we have revealed Street's counseling we ask a simple question: What would you think of a man or a woman who would personally say to you the things that are revealed in Street's counseling of the couple? Wouldn't you think it was rude, unkind, and unloving to speak about a spouse that way? Also, what would you think of Street setting such unbiblical standards for others to follow as he does in his position as head of the MABC at TMU&S? And, what would you think of broadcasting it to the whole world as Street does?

We asked at the beginning: Is the highly touted, popular, and influential biblical counseling program at The Master's University and Seminary truly biblical? Our answer is an emphatic No! for the reasons listed in this article as well as elsewhere.[17]

A Critical Review of The Master's University & Seminary Biblical Counseling Program

Part Three

In Part One of this chapter we demonstrate that the biblical counseling program at The Master's University and Seminary (TMU&S) is not truly biblical. Here in Part Three we reveal two egregious errors on the part of Street, which discredits his counseling.

Two More Serious Errors

In addition to Street's unbiblical problem-centered, sin-saturated counseling, we are concerned about two other areas of erroneous teaching, which have been widely spread through the audios and videos made of the

Biblical Counseling & Discipleship Association (BCDASoCal) Training Conference, Southern California, Fall 2011.[18] The first egregious teaching has to do with information Street gave to Julie about her depression and the other is his teaching about schizophrenia.

In speaking with Julie, Street says:

> Now, we know that there are certain types of diseases and circumstances that can bring on feelings of depression, symptoms of depression. **But all of those types of problems are easily discernible with a good, thorough physical. We know that**.... And let's assume that all the blood tests and everything that the Ob-Gyn has given you have turned out well. I mean, there's no sign of any organic abnormalities that's going on in you.... If the Ob-Gyn has jotted down a thorough job then **we can say that this is not organically caused**. The etiology or the very core of this causes the problem of **this is not an organic issue. It doesn't have to do with Julie's physiological body**, other than the fact that you're going through normal changes with pregnancy and a lot of changes going on in your life (bold added).[19]

Street's counseling is predicated on his belief that bodily diseases are "easily discernible" with "a good thorough physical" and his assumption that Julie had one. Street concludes with "**there's no sign of any organic abnormalities**" (bold added). According to Street, Julie's depression is "not an organic issue." He proceeds to counsel her based upon his questionable conclusion. Unfortunately there are many biblical counselors, such as

Street, who hold to the medically mistaken belief that a thorough medical exam in which no bodily disorders are found for depression indicates that there are no physical causes underlying or contributing to the depression and thus one can proceed to "cure" the depression biblically.

Street is apparently ignorant of the psychiatric treatment of mental disorders over the years, including depression, which turned out later to be true bodily disorders even after having had a "good thorough physical." Street seems unfamiliar with medical history and current practice where various physical diseases in their emerging state or actual existence have, even with a "good thorough physical," been shown to have no medical markers and yet result in depression and other mental disorders.[20]

There is a whole class of diseases called "idiopathic." According to the dictionary, "Idiopathic is an adjective used primarily in medicine meaning arising spontaneously or from an obscure or unknown cause."[21] In other words, there are **no medical markers** yet discovered for such diseases; there are **only symptoms**. There are many such diseases of both body and brain that occur. There are idiopathic diseases of the body that are known only by their symptoms. A *Wall Street Journal* article titled "Confusing Medical Ailments with Mental Illness" begins by saying, "More than 100 medical disorders can masquerade as psychological conditions or contribute to them, complicating treatment decisions."[22]

The article lists a number of these either-not-diagnosed or misdiagnosed bodily illnesses that result in depression and other mental symptoms. The article states: "Recognizing an underlying medical condition can be particularly difficult when there is also a psychological explanation for a patient's dark mood."[23] Or, we would add, when a biblical counselor such as Street assumes that a person's dark mood is due to a spiritual problem just because no bodily markers are found.

After giving reasons to contradict what Street teaches about being able to rule out possible biological problems that could lead to depression, since these are "easily discernible with a good, thorough physical," a medical doctor with extensive experience in the medical field comments, "Now how can Street say that one is safe medically if they get a thorough physical? There are many maladies that do not show up for years and cannot be detected by even a 'thorough' physical."[24] Surely there are medical doctors at Grace Community Church, where Street is an elder, who would say likewise. This mentality, such as Street's, of depression being a spiritual problem if no medical markers are found in a "good thorough exam" has caused much personal harm to believers.

How sad it is when a Christian diagnoses a fellow believer's depression as spiritually caused when, indeed, there may be hidden biological reasons for the symptoms. In the absence of biological markers, spiritualizing a mental disorder and prescribing a biblical regimen as Street does can be as serious a mistake as biologizing a mental disorder and prescribing a drug, the reason being that following Street's conclusion about depression could induce guilt and greater spiritual suffering in even the most godly individuals. **Wouldn't it be much better to admit that one may not know what underlies an individual's depression and yet provide spiritual**

ministry that could help alleviate the personal suffering and promote spiritual growth?

Everything in life has spiritual overtones. However, everything in life is not necessarily the sole result of our spiritual choices, and that includes depression, which can be the result of genetics, hormones, illnesses, diseases, injuries, and circumstances, all of which can affect one's state of mind. And, of course one will respond to the issues of life biblically more and more as one grows in the spirit and matures in the faith. Therefore, one should seek to minister the things of the Spirit and build individuals up in the Word. Whether the problem is biological, spiritual, or both, believers may minister God's mercy, grace, and truth to fellow believers, because every occasion of suffering can be used for comfort and spiritual growth **unless the one who ministers thinks he can diagnose another person's heart attitude**. There must be much humility in personally ministering to those who are suffering, even if they have brought this suffering upon themselves.

Street's questionable conclusion will surely cause many depressed believers to feel guilty about their "spiritual lack" when they may be as spiritually sound as Street himself. Compounding this mistaken teaching is the fact that **Street is teaching a spiritually and medically dangerous idea to many others worldwide, who will propagate this serious error among their colleagues and counselees**.

This medical ignorance on Street's part will be repeated throughout the work of his students and others who watch his video or hear his audio messages, which are readily available world-wide. **Think about the pos-**

sible medical and even spiritual consequences of this erroneous teaching being foisted upon naïve counselees by those trained by Street.

Schizophrenia

A second egregious teaching given by Street at the Fall 2011 Training Conference is in a talk in which he discusses thirteen psychological labels and avoiding the use of them. One of the labels he discusses is that of "schizophrenia."[25] He begins by saying, **"schizophrenia is just a nice Greek word for people who believe that they have personalities talking in the back of their head."** To begin with, Street has over-simplified a complex and not completely understood condition that comes in a variety of forms. It might surprise Street to know that there are some schizophrenics who do not "believe that they have personalities talking in the back of their head." **His overly simplistic statement is medically appalling as any neuropsychiatric expert would tell him.**

Street then compounds his grievous error by saying, "**Actually working with schizophrenia's not hard at all**" (bold added). To demonstrate how simple it is to work with schizophrenics, Street begins by saying, "If this represented all the schizophrenics in the world [at this point he stretches his arms out wide], only this many [he holds his thumb and forefinger almost together] are really genuine true Christians." In other words, there are almost no "genuine true Christians" who suffer from schizophrenia. Since only the Holy Spirit would know how many are and are not Christians, **Street has obviously usurped the place of the Holy Spirit** as he presumes to have knowledge that there is only a small number of schizophrenics who are believers, and he does so on the flimsiest and false biblical standard as will be seen shortly. **Such certain knowledge belongs only to God.**

Street proceeds to tell how one can **cure** schizophrenics by saying:

> And of those people [schizophrenics] you have to settle one thing early. Who's going to define your reality for you? The voices in the back of your head or the Bible? What's God's Word say? If you can settle that issue early with this, you can't work with all these other people. All these schizophrenics think that they're Christian; they're not. But you'd only work with a Christian. Remember all counseling is pre-counseling until a person comes to Christ. Right? Well, if you can settle that issue early: Who defines your reality for you? Is it what's God's Word says or is it that voice in the back of your head that says hurt yourself or hurt that other person.

So all one needs to do is to make sure the schizophrenic is a Christian because, according to Street, "you'd only work with a Christian" and "if you can settle that issue early" and "who defines reality for you… God's Word" or "that voice in the back of your head," then and only then a possible easy cure. While teaching people to base their reality on God's Word is sound advice, Street overlooks the complexity of schizophrenia and its range of symptoms.

Schizophrenia is one of the most enigmatic of the mental disorders and its **cure** has been elusive to this day. **For Street to casually set aside the billions-plus dollars spent and the multitudinous hours labored**

on research on schizophrenia by brilliant minds in his promotion of his personal opinion based on his proposed schizophrenia cure restricted to only an extremely small group of Christians that one is able to identify is reprehensible!

Harvard Medical School reports: "One in a hundred persons will at some time suffer from schizophrenia. **Its causes are obscure, and no way is known to prevent or cure it**"[26] (bold added).

In his book *Surviving Schizophrenia*, E. Fuller Torrey, MD, refers to schizophrenia as "today's most misunderstood illness" and says:

> Contrary to the popular stereotype, schizophrenia is an eminently treatable disease. That is not to say it is a curable disease, and the two should not be confused. Successful treatment means the control of symptoms, whereas cure means the permanent removal of their causes. Curing schizophrenia will not become possible until we understand its causes; in the meantime we must continue improving its treatment.[27]

Street's "cure" for "Christian" schizophrenics is based upon his say-so and could never be put to the scientific test; how could it be? To begin with, who or what establishes a person as a Christian, when Street says, "All these schizophrenics think that they're Christian; they're not"? Consider the amount of confusion and guilt that Street's blundering opinion will cause Christians who already suffer from schizophrenia.

Just as Street erroneously justifies his use of the Bible to support his unbiblical problem-centered counseling, he also erroneously uses the Bible to support his corrupt medical understanding of schizophrenia and his supposed cure. Consider the person with schizophrenia being counseled by Street or by someone he has trained who tries unsuccessfully to follow Street's plan, is not "biblically cured," and ends up concluding that he is willfully hearing "voices in the back of [his] head" and/or that he is eternally lost and rejected by God. Think of what might happen to one who not only continues to be plagued by voices, but enters into deep despair. **Hopefully Street's counseling and that of those who follow his teachings will not increase the suicide rate among those who suffer from schizophrenia.**

Imagine all those MABC students and those world-wide who see or hear Street's presentation on schizophrenia believing this egregiously false teaching and then counseling their counselees accordingly. These counselors will erroneously assume that **all** schizophrenics "have personalities talking in the back of their head[s]" and that the counselor merely needs to determine whether the counselee is a Christian and proceed to lead the counselee to listen to God instead—and then: **"abracadabra," a cure! And, imagine the potential lawsuits that may occur because of this teaching carried out by Street and all these biblical counselors who follow him.** This is one more tragedy of Street's false teaching that is available at TMU&S and the BCDASoCal web site for anyone in the world to see and hear and erroneously believe and follow. Because of Street's position and background and because Dr. John MacArthur, who heads TMU&S, is so highly regarded world-wide, many will embrace these teachings.

Torrey versus Street

E. Fuller Torrey, M.D, quoted earlier, is a research psychiatrist specializing in depressive illness and schizophrenia. Torrey is the executive director of the Stanley Medical Research Institute and has written several important best-selling books on mental illness. Torrey is an eminent research authority, who has over many years seen numerous patients suffering from depressive illness and schizophrenia. Therefore, we were interested in Torrey's response to Street's teaching on depression and schizophrenia.

We were also interested in Torrey's medical response to Street's belief that bodily diseases are "easily discernible" with "a good thorough physical" and to Street's conclusion that in Julie's case "there is no sign of any organic abnormalities." In addition, we were curious as to what Torrey would say about Street's views on schizophrenia. Torrey responded to us as follows:

> Dr. Street's advice betrays a woeful lack of knowledge. Depression and many other psychiatric disorders are physical diseases of the brain which are not detectable by "a good, thorough physical," including blood tests. Psychiatric disorders can be caused by genetic, infectious, metabolic, and other organic etiologies, some of which are detectable by a physical exam and blood tests, but **many cannot be**.
>
> His [Street's] statement about schizophrenia is simply ignorant. I have known many "true Christians" who have schizophrenia. **The fact that Dr.**

> **Street is in a teaching position is scandalous**[28] (bold added).

Recommendations

Prior to the current biblical counseling program, The Master's University had a Behavioral Studies Program. At that time we were still involved in and promoted the biblical counseling movement. We thought it would be wonderful if the Behavioral Studies Program would be replaced by a biblical counseling program and even strongly recommended that it be done. Eventually it was decided to replace the Behavioral Studies Program with a biblical counseling program, and Dr. Bob Smith from Faith Baptist Counseling Ministries was hired for two years to establish the program. After Smith's two-year stint, Dr. Wayne Mack of the Christian Counseling and Educational Foundation was employed to carry on. Street is the current head.

During this period of time, after considerable soul searching and discussions with trusted friends (some of whom disagreed with us), we wrote and published *Against Biblical Counseling: For the Bible* (*ABC*). We did not come to the conclusions contained within that book quickly or easily. And, we did not expect those immersed in the biblical counseling movement to make an about-face. We believe that many never will. Subsequent to writing *ABC*, we wrote *Christ-Centered Ministry versus Problem-Centered Counseling; Person to Person Ministry: Soul Care in the Body of Christ;* and *Stop Counseling! Start Ministering!*

We are making the following two recommendations to right the wrong that exists in the biblical

counseling master's degree program (MABC) at The Master's University and Seminary:

1. Replace the MABC program with a Behavioral Studies program with the emphasis on a scientific understanding of the broad field of psychology and particularly with an exposé of the field of clinical psychology out of which come the psychotherapists and other psychological counselors. This would arm students for the battles that will occur after they leave The Master's University and Seminary and protect them from looking over their shoulders at what the world has to offer.

2. Encourage the current MABC students to enroll in a Biblical Studies program with special emphasis on ministering versus counseling. The major could be called Biblical Ministry Master of Arts (BMMA). It would give those students who are called to personal biblical care a strong foundation in Scripture to help them minister the Word of God in love and truth with the focus on our Lord Jesus Christ.

6

Dr. Jim Newheiser

The IBCD website describes Newheiser as follows:

> Dr. James (Jim) Newheiser, Jr., is the Director of the Institute for Biblical Counseling and Discipleship (IBCD) and the Director of the Christian Counseling Program at RTS [Reformed Theological Seminary] Charlotte. He is also the Associate Professor of Christian Counseling and Practical Theology at RTS Charlotte and an Adjunct Professor of Biblical Counseling at The Master's University. Furthermore, Dr. Newheiser serves as a board member at both the Biblical Counseling Coalition (BCC) and the Association of Certified Biblical Counselors (ACBC). For 25 years, Dr. Newheiser served as the Preaching Pastor at Grace Bible Church in Escondido, California before taking over the Christian Counseling Program at RTS Charlotte in 2016. He now oversees all the counseling degree options, including the 66 credit-hour MA in Christian Counseling (MACC).[1]

As we said in Chapter 4, the Institute for Biblical Counseling & Discipleship (IBCD) has a Core & Discipleship Certification (CDC) Program, which is "designed to help churches develop one another care in the life of the congregation." One can be certified by IBCD, and "The CDC process also brings one along towards the ACBC [Association of Certified Biblical Counselors] Certification if further certification is desired."[2]

We say categorically, and have demonstrated from our past writings, that for various reasons **we recommend against becoming a certificated biblical counselor**.[3] We have often explained many of the reasons why we left the biblical counseling movement (BCM).[4] One of the key reasons is that those in the BCM, including the IBCD counselors, are problem-centered, in that they often talk about problems in a manner similar to those in the psychological counseling movement. **Biblical counseling as generally conducted by IBCD is nowhere found in Scripture.**[5] As mentioned earlier, Dr. David Powlison affirmed that the use of biblical counseling as done in the BCM is newly arrived in the church.[6] As we often say, **if the psychological counseling movement did not exist, the biblical counseling movement would not have followed in its footsteps of problem-centered sinful conversations in which it currently exists.**

We assume that Newheiser would be considered among the very best and ablest to show prospective certificate students how biblical counseling can best be conducted. We also assume that Newheiser is the *ne plus ultra* of what IBCD expects those trained by him to emulate.

A statement preceding Newheiser's counseling reveals that the "observation sessions are fictional but based on real life scenarios." In other words, they are imaginative reconstructions "based on real life scenarios." Newheiser's counseling cases are clearly not scripted. However, when we called the IBCD office we were told that the counselors and their "counselees" were "playacting and one of them [Dan] is a professional actor."[7] These are obviously contrived cases with predictable successes, or why else would they be offered? Since some of the acting is quite convincing, the viewer might even forget that these are simply artful presentations that lack the literal live dialog of real live cases and thereby erroneously conclude that real cases look like what is seen in these contrived presentations. **As we often say, anything less than a literal live case with literal live dialog is less than the literal live truth.**

When watching these playacted counseling cases, be mindful of the obvious pinned-on microphones and the fact that each DVD has likely been put together over many hours to create a smooth-looking final result. As often occurs with biblical counselors, these scenes include a combination of excellent Bible teaching eclipsed by unbiblical sinful dialogue on which the counseling depends.

The *Care & Discipleship Resource Handbook*[8] from the *IBCD Observation 12-Disc Set* provides a "Personal Data Inventory" (PDI) form, which is completed by each counselee. The PDI requires answers to "Background Information," "Health Information," "Religious Background," "Marriage and Family Information," and "Personality Information." Christians ministered to one another prior to the creation and use of the PDI, and they were in no way hampered or restricted by the non-use of a PDI. We again emphasize that using the PDI would more likely subtract from, rather than add to, the counseling process; because it is totally unnecessary and will often provide distractions from the real needs. Furthermore, the PDI stimulates negative thinking about others and evil speaking about other people. Nevertheless, the PDI and other such inventories are considered to be valuable by problem-centered counselors, even though they would be a detriment when ministering biblically.

Unbiblical Errors in Jim Newheiser Cases

There are several major unbiblical errors in Jim Newheiser's counseling cases, which we will expose. The first is speaking unbiblically about a spouse who is not present as in the case of "Jesse" and a spouse who is present as in the case of "Dan & Debbie"; and finally, discussing the marriage bed relationship, as in the cases of "Jesse" in the absence of his wife and "Dan" in the presence of his wife, "Debbie," which is most egregiously unbiblical and most reflective of the world and the sinful extent to which biblical counselors will go.

"Jesse"

The first case is Newheiser counseling Jesse. Although there is much good Bible teaching by Newheiser, his teaching is eclipsed by his unbiblical excursions into Jesse's personal life and private relationships. We will give a brief glimpse of why others should not emulate this aspect of his counseling.

When Newheiser asks why Jesse came to him, Jesse begins by saying that his biggest problem is at work and confesses that his wife caused him to come. The conversation then biblically deteriorates into Newheiser probing into private relationship areas and Jesse responding to him. Jesse confesses, "No matter how much I do, it's not enough." Newheiser asks, "Not enough for who [sic]?" Jesse complains about his wife and Newheiser probes for details. Newheiser asks about any crisis or arguments that caused Jesse's wife to urge him to come. Newheiser also explores arguments between Jesse and his wife.

Referring to his wife, Jesse says, "It's been years since she's been happy—or we've had fun." Jesse says, "Life has sort of slipped into this routine…." Newheiser interrupts and offers, "You kind of feel like you're a hamster on a wheel." Jesse responds, "Yeah, yeah, you know." Jesse confesses that he and his wife "fight about stuff." Newheiser explores the details of Jesse and Sarah's arguments, sympathizes with Jesse, and states, "If your wife was just happy to be married to you and appreciative of you, that would make such a difference." Jesse responds, "Yeah, right." Jesse describes a plate incident and says, "I get read the riot act because I didn't rinse a plate."

Throughout the three counseling sessions with Jesse, Newheiser asks, probes, seeks, and even leads Jesse into revealing as much as possible about himself, his wife, and their personal relationships. Jesse is sinning against Sarah in her absence by exposing what he regards as her sinful behavior to a third party. In addition to failing to show love to Sarah in her absence, Jesse says hurtful things about her and singles her out as the major reason for his own unhappiness.

We know that those in the psychological counseling movement function as Newheiser does, but what does the Bible say about how we are to speak in conversation, particularly in reference to others? One might begin with the following Scriptures:

> But I say unto you, That every idle word that men shall speak, they shall give account thereof in the day of judgment. For by thy words thou shalt be justified, and by thy words thou shalt be condemned. (Matt. 12:36-37.)
>
> Charity suffereth long, and is kind; charity envieth not; charity vaunteth not itself, is not puffed up, doth not behave itself unseemly, seeketh not her own, is not easily provoked, thinketh no evil; rejoiceth not in iniquity, but rejoiceth in the truth; beareth all things, believeth all things, hopeth all things, endureth all things. (1 Cor. 13:4-7.)
>
> Let no corrupt communication proceed out of your mouth, but that which is good to the use of edifying, that it may minister grace unto the hearers. (Eph. 4:29.)
>
> For this cause shall a man leave his father and mother, and shall be joined unto his wife, and they two shall be one flesh. This is a great mystery: but I speak concerning Christ and the church. Nevertheless let every one of you in particular so love his wife even as himself; and the wife see that she reverence her husband. (Eph. 5:31-33)

Newheiser asks obliquely about Jesse and his wife's sex life. Jesse confirms that they "come together" sexually "twice a month." Newheiser asks, "Is that something you're both pleased with?" Jesse responds, "I don't think she cares." "It's always like a chore I think for her and that's frustrating." Newheiser affirms, "You don't want to feel like you're a bother?" Jesse responds,

"I don't want to be with someone who is like doing it begrudgingly."

This excursion into the privacy of Jesse and Sarah's sexual intimacy is unholy at least and unbiblical at worst. The marriage bed is holy and for Newheiser to pry and for Jesse to expose his wife in the way he does is seriously sinful, but Newheiser is the one who, in his authoritative role as counselor (one-up), has precipitated and therefore encouraged Jesse's unfaithful and unmerciful responses (one-down). In addition to the prior verses regarding conversation, Ephesians 5:25–29 says:

> Husbands, love your wives, even as Christ also loved the church, and gave himself for it; That he might sanctify and cleanse it with the washing of water by the word, that he might present it to himself a glorious church, not having spot, or wrinkle, or any such thing; but that it should be holy and without blemish. So ought men to love their wives as their own bodies. He that loveth his wife loveth himself. For no man ever yet hated his own flesh; but nourisheth and cherisheth it, even as the Lord the church.

There is a final session with both Jesse and Sarah, his wife. Newheiser first says to Sarah, "Just wanted to explain to you what's going on." Newheiser then asks, "Has he [Jesse] been sharing with you what we have been talking about? Sarah nods a "yes" answer. This appears to bc an incrcdible question and response that lack credibility! Is anyone naïve enough to believe that Jesse has revealed to Sarah all the unbiblical bad-mouthing he poured into Newheiser's receptive ears? Add to this that Newheiser has been this couple's pastor for three years.

Review all the critical and caustic statements made by Jesse about Sarah during counseling and think about the possibility that he would reveal his outrageous talk about her behind her back when he got home.

Newheiser then goes on to explain some details of the two prior sessions with Jesse. Newheiser says, "Application here would be I've heard kind of about him from him—Jesse from Jesse—but someone else—the person who is closest to him—has a different perspective. I'm not saying it is contradictory, but sometimes we don't even know ourselves as well as we think we do." Newheiser's summary of his prior counseling of Jesse omitted Jesse's criticism of Sarah and even his revealing to Newheiser, when asked obliquely how often they had been "coming together," their twice-a-month sexual intimacy. In all candor, Proverbs 18:17 would require that all of Jesse's allegations about Sarah be brought out into the open so she can respond to them. That would be the biblical obligation that Newheiser would have, but failed to do.

In spite of so much focus having been on Sarah's faults during the first two sessions, Newheiser says to Sarah, "I want to assure you that when I am counseling a man by himself, my only purpose is not to tell him what his wife did wrong but to focus on him." While Newheiser did not tell Jesse what Sarah did wrong, he permitted and even encouraged Jesse to talk about Sarah's wrongs through his questions and sympathetic responses—**a grossly unbiblical thing to do**!

"Dan & Debbie"

Newheiser and his wife, Caroline Newheiser, are counseling Dan and Debbie in this enacted case. The acting on the part of Dan, a professional actor, is commendable, **but the counseling primarily done by Jim is lamentable. To portray this as a successful counseling case to others sets a standard of practice that should not be followed**, as it could easily lead to the husband not coming back or, even worse, to increased conflict and bitterness between Dan and Debbie and maybe a divorce.

Marriage counseling is big business in the world and in the church. As more and more people have been going to marriage counseling, more and more have become divorced, and this includes professing Christians, who may be divorcing at about the same rate as unbelievers.[9] With all the time and money and the great expectations that counseling will help married couples, it is disconcerting to learn that marriage counseling only helps about half of the time, which is similar to sham treatment. Why are the results so poor? We repeat here what the editor of *Psychotherapy Networker,* a journal for practicing psychotherapists, confesses: "most therapists who actually do marital therapy (about 80 percent of all clinicians) don't really know what they're doing." He says:

> Untrained in and unprepared for work that requires a highly skilled touch and nerves of steel, many therapists blunder ineffectually through sessions until they're fired by their clients or, overwhelmed by a couple's problems, they give up too soon in trying to save a marriage.[10]

But then he admits that skilled, experienced therapists are often unsuccessful as well. One psychotherapist reported in a professional journal article that:

> Controlled outcome studies show that only about half of couples improve with treatment. And even among those who do make progress, a disheartening chunk, 30 to 50 percent, relapse within two years.[11]

Blaming the Past

Exploring the past is one of the major themes of Freudian and other insight-oriented psychotherapies. Permitting and participating in such problem-centered counseling is clearly unbiblical (Phil. 3:13, 14). As a result of the PDI, it is revealed that Newheiser indulges in an unbiblical error of focusing on early life influences when reporting about Dan and Debbie.

Newheiser says:

> Dan's father died when he was young and he was raised by a strict mom. Debbie grew up with non-Christian parents and had lots of freedom. Dan does not like being counseled and has some years of anger "bottled up." Debbie believes that she is doing the right thing.[12]

For years many in the biblical counseling movement have dealt with problems of living by talking about the problems, feelings, circumstances, and the sins of others, including family members. Because many psychological counseling theories consider one's childhood to be the source of later problems, much time may be devoted to looking for ways that parents and other adults failed to give the child exactly what the counselee or counselor thinks the child needed at the time.

There is no biblical basis for such use of the past (as determinants of present behavior). The Bible includes the past works of God in history, because we are to remember the works of God both individually and corporately. But, regarding the Christian walk, the cross took care of the past. The walk of the believer is to be according to the new life and is therefore present and future oriented. In Philippians 3 Paul gives his religious and personal background, on which he had depended for righteousness before God. But when confronted by Jesus he saw his own wretched sinfulness, not only that he had persecuted the church, but that he was sinful to the core. He knew he could not make himself righteous by going back into his past. Therefore he declared: "This one thing I do, forgetting those things which are behind, and reaching forth unto those things which are before, I press toward the mark for the prize of the high calling of God in Christ Jesus" (Phil. 3:13-14). This does not mean an inability to recall the past; it means that the past now has a different significance. Biblically speaking, attempting to fix the past is purely a fleshly activity that wars against the Spirit.

A person need not be trapped in negative patterns of behavior established in the early years of life, for the Bible offers a new way of life. Put off the old man; put on the new. Jesus said to Nicodemus, "Ye must be born again" (John 3:7), and He said elsewhere that new wine could not be put into old wineskins (Matt. 9:17). Jesus offers new life and new beginnings. One who is born again has the spiritual capacity to overcome old ways and develop new ones through the action of the Holy Spirit, the fruit of the Spirit, and the sanctification of the believer. One wonders why so many have given up the hope of Christianity for the hopelessness of past determinism.

Turning to the past to find reasons for present problems, as often happens in problem-centered counseling, places blame on others and on circumstances rather than on one's own responsibilities and possibilities. Because of the nature of memory, remembering the past cannot be done without enhancing, embellishing, omitting, or creating details to fill in the blanks.[13] Therefore, this is a faulty method of help because of the brain's limited ability to remember accurately and its tendency to distort.

Christ dealt with every believer's past at the cross when he died for their sins. When believers by grace through faith identify with Christ's death and resurrection they are free from the past of the flesh as well as the power of the flesh. They have a new life in Christ and are to live according to that new life. **Attempts to heal the hurts of the past are futile because one is not to heal that which is to be counted dead and buried.** Such sinful attempts give power to the flesh and will result in fleshly living in place of walking according to the Spirit. **Christ-centered ministry will encourage and help a seeker to leave the past at the foot of the cross and to "press toward the mark for the prize of the high calling of God in Christ Jesus"** (Phil. 3:14).

This past and parental blame for one's current state of mind is now even being questioned among some psychotherapists. An article in a professional psychotherapy journal states:

> Perhaps the most enduring but unsubstantiated theoretical belief among therapists is the time-worn notion that difficulties in adulthood stem from childhood misfortunes. Almost all therapy approaches, from psychoanalysis and Imago therapy to the emotion-focused and sensorimotor methods, embrace some version of this dogma. Given its venerable pedigree, this belief in the potency of childhood events is one of the most difficult to deconstruct. Nevertheless, as a general clinical hypothesis, it's deeply flawed.
>
> The simple truth is that a preponderance of the evidence mitigates [militates] against assigning any great importance to childhood experiences and memories—processed, unprocessed, or re-processed. Martin Seligman, the former president of the American Psychological Association, puts it this way: "Childhood events—even childhood trauma—and childrearing appear to have only weak effects on adult life. Childhood, contrary to popular belief, does not seem, empirically, to be particularly formative. So, contrary to popular belief, we are not prisoners of our past."[14]

The journal also states:

> Most therapists like exploring feelings with their clients, delving into family history, helping them achieve emotional growth, going deep—and taking their time doing it. That's why they got into therapy in the first place.[15]

Replace "therapists" and "therapy" with "counselors" and "counseling" and likewise it can be said of many of those in the BCM.

Three Serious Errors

Because of the human tendency to blame others, the first serious error is to counsel such a couple together. The hostility and anger voiced by Dan to "third" parties will only, under normal versus contrived counseling circumstances, drive a deeper wedge into the relationship. For Dan to play the victim while exposing his wife personally is reprehensible and irresponsible. For Jim to permit such theatrics for others to follow is biblically erroneous.

The second more serious error is for Jim to follow Dan, who brought up the subject, into the marriage bed. Dan alleges that Debbie is obsessed with cleanliness in the house and that she has been withholding sex from him. Dan's description of Debbie's reluctance is not only critical but also mocking at times. Dan sarcastically says, "I'm not the one withholding sex from my wife," meaning, of course, that she is the one depriving him. Dan then jabs deeper by saying, "I'm not withholding sex because the house isn't clean." By getting into the topic of sex, Jim opens the door for Dan to sin against his wife by ridiculing her in an area which should be kept private. In doing so Dan acts as a talebearer who "reveals secrets; but he that is of a faithful spirit concealeth the matter" (Prov. 11:13).

As Jim pursues the sexual intimacy subject, he attempts to bring some balance by saying, "In Matthew 7 Jesus says, after you get the log out of your eye, then you're able to see clearly to take what's in her eye out of her eye." But Dan has been given so much freedom to insult his wife that he is not ready for correction. In fact, he overrides Jim's one-up position and says: "So what's my log? I don't demand sex or I shouldn't expect it?" Later Dan asks, "How does me wanting my wife to come upstairs—how is that wrong for me to expect that and how is it right for her to stay downstairs cleaning the house from cover to cover?" After Jim's reading and discussing James 4, Dan asks, "It's okay for me to desire to be in bed with my wife?" Then after a brief interchange, Dan says, "If her body is mine and she's not providing it [sexual intimacy] because of some stupid ideas…that the house has to be…." This kind of counseling permits a husband to verbally expose the person he is called to love and protect (Eph. 5:25-28; 1 Peter 3:7). Just as with psychological counseling, one spouse looks to the counselor to judge the situation and thereby make the other spouse change through intimidation or guilt induction.

In the third counseling meeting the subject of sex comes up early. Dan reports, "She didn't come upstairs to bed. If she forgave me, she would have come up right away." Jim asks, "Did it finally happen?" meaning, did they finally have sexual intimacy. Dan confirms that it did "finally happen." Dan expresses his desperate desire for sex by saying, "If it doesn't happen I go nuts." A few minutes later Dan laments, "I don't think that a husband should beg a wife to go to bed."

Our earlier criticisms of Jim's biblical violations when counseling Jesse doubly apply here with Dan and Debbie, because of the unnecessary sexual excursion and diversion. Such excursions into this sensitive and biblically sacred area of marriage by biblical counselors are not unusual. Jim is only doing what is standard for many counselors and probably what he teaches others to do.[16] As we say about such needless excursions: This reveals how deeply worldly this counseling is and the extent to which psychological problem-centered counseling with its sinful conversations has been emulated and embraced by biblical counselors. As much as prying for details is expected and practiced in biblical counseling, details about a couple's sexual intimacy should not be shared with a third party or pursued by a biblical counselor. Nevertheless problem-centered counseling, such as practiced and encouraged by Jim, depends on such details, even in these intimate areas. There are ways to minister to couples without invading their bedrooms and physical intimacy through unnecessary and unhelpful sinful communication.

Jim's excursion into the privacy of Dan and Debbie's sexual intimacy is a reflection of psychological counseling rather than a biblical need. While the topic of sex is clearly dealt with in Scripture, Paul was teaching in 1 Corinthians 7, rather than having private sessions with couples during which they exposed one another! One does not need to hear the complaints or the details to teach about marriage. Biblical counselors would do well to skip the preliminaries (the digging and prying) and teach the doctrines and principles from Scripture, thereby **trusting the Holy Spirit to do the convicting and the inner work for outer obedience**.

Conclusion

Over the years we have heard and seen a number of biblical counseling cases acted out as in the IBCD Observations or described as in *Counseling the Hard Cases*.[17] We have continually complimented the excellent, at times, teachings that are presented, but, in spite of the fact that those in the BCM are often biblical in their teaching of Scripture, they are biblically undone by what they do in their counseling. **In other words, their counseling betrays their intent to be biblical, as we continually reveal.**

What we say may shock some and be a relief to others, but it is entirely unnecessary to take biblical counseling classes in order to be effectively used by God to minister godly counsel to one another along the way to Christian maturity. A disagreement we would have with the biblical counseling training program promoters, such as IBCD, is that they attempt to prepare individuals to be "biblical counselors," such as Newheiser, when he should prepare individuals to do biblical ministry as part of the biblically ordained ministries found in Ephesians 4:11–16, Romans 12, and elsewhere in Scripture. One needs to "Study to show thyself approved unto God, a workman that needeth not to be ashamed, rightly dividing the word of truth" (2 Timothy 2:15). Such study occurs in worship services, Bible studies, Sunday school classes, and at other times of reading and instruction in the Word, but it is often absent in the biblical counseling movement because of its sinful conversations.

We repeat, the biblical counseling movement is a recent phenomenon in church history. **The certificate/ degree training programs are entirely unnecessary to**

minister effectively to individuals, couples, and families. These were not necessary before the latter-day invention of the biblical counseling movement and they are totally unnecessary now. The certificate/degree-oriented biblical counseling organizations act as intimidators and disablers of mature believers who would, with a little encouragement, minister to fellow believers in need. This smacks of an one-up/one-down relationship. From our many years of experience, we know that there are numerous Christians who are mature in the faith who would be blessed to minister to others in the fellowship, but who do not because they feel blockbustered by one-up training organizations and educational institutions that promote training followed by more training.

As more and more biblical counseling organizations spring up and as more and more training in biblical counseling is recommended, there will be fewer and fewer mature believers ministering, because they will be more and more intimidated if they have not been trained. **So the idea of more biblical counselors being available by getting more believers trained will actually result in fewer and fewer believers who are mature in the faith ministering to one another in the Body of Christ**. The objective of biblical counseling training may be to have more individuals available for counseling, but they are discouraging far more people from ministry than they are training, and thus the problem is worsened by the training programs.

The idea of the need for training believers in counseling actually results in believers concluding that they are unable to minister unless they have been sufficiently trained (more and more courses and manuals), supervised, degreed, certificated, and instructed through manuals with contrived counseling cases and special methodologies. In a word, they are intimidated. By shutting down the biblical training programs with their accompanying intimidation, more and more mature believers would begin to minister if encouraged to do so.

We challenge these institutions that claim to put the Word first to test what we have said according to the very Word they claim to defend. We challenge them to biblically defend the literal detailed dialogues that occur in what is called biblical counseling. As we said earlier, although we are opposed to Christians enrolling in any certificate or degree biblical counseling programs to learn such systems and methods of counseling, **we do encourage those who wish to minister to others to increase their Bible knowledge, to attend Bible classes, or to enroll in a biblical studies degree program rather than a biblical counseling degree program.**

There are numerous biblical counseling books in print and few that have detailed counseling conversations; thus, **we recommend that one withhold judgment about a particular biblical counseling approach, such as IBCD, until one knows exactly what kinds of conversations go on in the counseling, whether sinful or godly.** And note particularly how often or seldom sinful talk and behavior are called "sinful" in their conversations. If such information is not provided, then that should eliminate that approach from consideration. Based upon these many counseling conversations that we have examined over many years, we find that the biblical counseling cases are highly problem-centered, sin-saturated, and therefore very unbiblical.

The principles and practices of biblical counseling certificate organizations weaken the position of the church, the role of pastors, the role of church leaders, and especially the ability of lay people to minister to one another. We have, in our training and calling others to mutual care ministry, ignored certificates and degrees in biblical counseling and emphasized the importance of finding believers who (1) are knowledgeable in the Word, (2) are filled and gifted by the Holy Spirit to minister to others, (3) have shown through their behavior that they are growing in sanctification, (4) and have walked with the Lord and been dependent upon Him through their trials in life. Such knowledge, life, gifts, and callings become apparent as believers come to know one another in the Body of Christ in the local church. Increasing one's knowledge of the Bible is essential, but biblical counseling, as preached by those in the certificate/degree organizations can be detrimental.

7

Dr. Paul Tripp

Dr. Paul David Tripp earned his M.Div. from Reformed Episcopal Seminary and his D.Min in Biblical Counseling from Westminster Theological Seminary. After studying biblical counseling at Westminster, Tripp became a faculty member of the Christian Counseling & Educational Foundation (CCEF) and a lecturer in biblical counseling at Westminster. He was a pastor at Tenth Presbyterian Church in Philadelphia and in 2006 he started Paul Tripp Ministries. From this base he is a much sought-out speaker.[1]

Tripp is very popular, both as a speaker and writer, particularly among those who are interested in what is called "biblical counseling" and "discipleship." Although he may sound biblical, much of what he is teaching, promoting, and popularizing is the problem-centered, idols-of-the-heart counseling methodology, which has been recycled from psychological insight-oriented counseling methodology and integrated with the Bible by CCEF. As we indicated in Chapter 3, David Powlison is the godfather of this latter day mania, but **Tripp's writings are an excellent example of idols-of-the-heart counseling recycled from insight-oriented psychotherapy.**

The way Tripp connects the heart with the motives and then endeavors to give the counselee insight into his own heart is very similar to a psychoanalytic therapist's attempt to expose the hidden regions of the unconscious with its so-called unconscious determinants of behavior. Psychoanalytic methods of insight and interpretation lead to much subjective guessing as the therapist analyzes what the counselee reveals about herself. Nevertheless, insight-oriented therapists and idols-of-the-heart counselors truly believe that, as they listen to what the person says, they will be able to know and reveal to their counselees their inner core (heart) and what drives them.

Distorting Doctrines

Typical of CCEF books and articles, Paul Tripp's writings include some good teaching. Tripp emphasizes the heart, the inner man, and teaches some truths about the war between the flesh and the Spirit and about how human beings are in rebellion against their creator and end up serving and worshipping self. Therefore, one will find much to agree with. However, **these truths make the book more dangerous**, because of the way he engages the readers with truth, but is ever so subtly leading them into his problem-centered and thus self-centered, insight-oriented counseling methodology. Tripp gives the impression that mere humans can know another person's heart if they are especially trained in the elitist idols-of-the-heart counseling methodology. **Tripp's book *Instruments in the Redeemer's Hands* (*IRH*),[2] written to help counselors see and expose deceitful hearts, is itself a masterpiece of deception as it weaves biblical teachings with recycled insight-oriented psychotherapy.** Scripture is treated as if it must be aided by the counselor's insight to be effective—as if it must be insight infused in addition to being God breathed. Tripp is facile in his method of syncretizing psychology with Scripture in such a way as to disguise the strong psychotherapeutic theories and methods lying beneath his biblical-sounding explanations.

Tripp is quite typical of CCEF in his problem-centeredness and analytical idols-of the-heart methodology, which is limited to working with the old man or the flesh since **only God truly knows anyone's deceitful heart.** And this is the crux of the matter. Are believers going to examine and attempt to change a heart filled with idolatrous desires, which can only belong to what Scripture calls "the old man" or the "flesh"? Or are they going to put off the old man every time it raises it ugly head through either internal or external expression?

Tripp and others in the idols-of-the-heart insight camp will say that they are helping people to walk according to their new life in Christ, but their psychologically inspired methodology is limited to the flesh. Christ's life in the believer, through the indwelling Holy Spirit, does not have idols. Any idols or forms of idolatry are limited to the old man or the flesh. To get rid of idols according to the idols-of-the-heart system, one must be searching out idols in the old man or the flesh. If self is central with the domination of the flesh, idols may be exchanged and shifted around in such a way that the person becomes even more deceived. Unless believers die to self by reckoning themselves dead to sin and alive to God (Romans 6:11), they are still under the wrong ruler, both inside and out.

Tripp's methodology has to do with seeking out the inner man, the heart. In answering the question of why people do what they do, Tripp quotes Luke 6:43-45 and says that "the roots of the tree equal the heart. They are underground and therefore not as easily seen or understood" (*IRH*, 61). He wants to discover the idols of the heart—the desires and motivations—just as insight-oriented psychotherapists attempt to search out the possible whys and wherefores of their counselees' behavior, with the belief that these hidden depths within the psyche are directing feelings, thoughts, and behavior outside conscious awareness.

Tripp's underlying idols-of-the-heart theory and method of counseling are reflective of psychotherapeutic methods of insight and interpretation. Insight oriented psychotherapy leads one into the most subjective realm of psychology, which was originally an offshoot of philosophy, and ends up being what Scripture calls "philosophy and vain deceit" (Col. 2:8), because this kind of psychology relies on much imagination, speculation, and subjectivity.

Delving, Digging, and Evil Speaking

The process of getting to know another person and what idols are controlling the person's life involves much digging, delving, and evil speaking about other people who may or not be present to defend themselves in this kangaroo-court proceeding. Tripp's article "Identity and Story: A Counseling Transcript," published in CCEF's *Journal of Biblical Counseling*, demonstrates what typically goes on in idols-of-the-heart counseling. The case involves a couple, Frank and Gina, with Tripp focusing on three things regarding Frank:

> 1. I wanted to hear his story in a bit of detail. The only way I can help them make sense out of the details of their story is if I also know those details....
>
> 2. I wanted to know how Frank and Gina were relating to one another in the middle of their trouble....
>
> 3. I wanted most of all for them to be able to look at the mess of their lives and see God, so they could begin to clean up the mess.[3]

Tripp evidently believes he must obtain lots of information (complaints) before he can minister, because he contends that he has to know a counselee's so-called idols of the heart. Tripp says, "If we fail to examine the heart and the areas where it needs to change, our ministry efforts will only result in people who are more committed and successful idolaters" (*IRH*, 68).

Tripp reveals what kind of information he is looking for in his attempt to know another person's heart in a section in *IRH* titled "Now For Some Good Questions" (*IRH*, 174ff). In the first item Tripp advises, "Always ask open-ended questions that cannot be answered with a 'yes' or 'no'" (*IRH*, p. 175). Following this he gives over 25 questions as examples. Here are several of his questions:

- What things in your marriage make you sad?
- How would you characterize your communication with your husband?

- Describe how you as a couple resolve conflicts.
- What do you see as the weaknesses of your marriage?
- What could your spouse do to greatly change your marriage?
- Pick one area of your marriage where you think you have problems. Describe what is wrong and what each of you has done to solve it. (*IRH,* 175-176)

One has to wonder how these might differ from secular marriage counseling. They are problem-loaded and will roil up the troubled waters with the husband and wife complaining, speaking ill of one another, and airing their dissatisfaction with the marriage and with one another to an attentive listener who is eager to know more about what's wrong. All through this kind of counseling, counselees are given many opportunities to violate numerous biblical admonitions, including Proverbs 11:13; 1 Corinthians 13:4-7; Ephesians 4:29; 5:22-33; 6:23; James 3:2-8; and 1 Peter 3:5-7. With this type of problem-centered counseling, filled with the expressions of the deceitful heart of the Jeremiah 17:9 syndrome,[4] it is understandable that some counseling goes on for over a year—possibly ending in divorce.

Counseling that relies on talking about problems and asking these kinds of questions will often lead counselees into violating Leviticus 19:16: "Thou shalt not go up and down as a talebearer among thy people: neither shalt thou stand against the blood of thy neighbour: I am the LORD." The amount of talebearing in counseling is excessive. In fact, **without such talebearing this kind**

of counseling would cease to exist, since it inevitably depends upon talebearing and speaking evil of others.

In his *IRH*, Tripp tells about Mike and Marsha who come to him for help. He says:

> Mike began to tell the most confusing family story I had ever heard. They had both been married before and had blended two families, each with four older children. Marsha occasionally jumped in with details that only added to my confusion. I don't think I took as many notes in my theology classes at seminary as I did that afternoon! Their story was full of plots and sub-plots. Their attempts to solve problems invariably made them worse. It seemed that their children had made all the wrong decisions as well. It *was* a mess! (*IRH*, 183, italics his.)

Such details provide for much blame-shifting and sinful speaking about other people. Problem-centered counselors thrive on hearing the "plots and sub-plots" and the messes in the lives of their counselees and therefore take many notes for future problem-centered counseling appointments, inevitably saturated with sinful conversations.

Confessing the Sins of Others

The cases Tripp discusses are filled with information that he could only have gleaned through eliciting gossip, complaints about others, and evil speaking about parents, spouse, and others. He appears to be blind to the fact that much of what he seeks to hear from the counselee is filled with self-exonerating gossip, since he himself clearly speaks out against gossip when he says:

> Gossip doesn't lead a person to make humble confession before God or others. When I gossip, I confess the sin of another person to someone **who is not involved**. Gossip doesn't restrain sin, it encourages it. It doesn't build someone's character; it destroys his reputation. Gossip doesn't lead a person to humble insight; it produces anger and defensiveness (*IRH*, 206, bold added).

We certainly agree with much of what he says here about gossip! However, he obviously allows such gossiping during counseling. Evidently, because he is in the role of counselor, he would naturally see himself as someone **who is involved**, rather than "someone **who is not involved**." This short phrase seemingly makes the counselor privy to all kinds of confessions of the sins of others without calling it "gossip." Through the questions he asks and by the information he has gleaned during hours of counseling with individuals, he depends on lots of what would ordinarily be called "gossip" (talebearing) and sinful evil speaking about others in his quest to know the hearts of his counselees. In his attempt to identify a person's so-called motivating idols of the heart, Tripp elicits self-disclosure, but what he is looking for will generally be contaminated with much self-protective bias, talebearing, and evil speaking about others. Here are some of his scenarios that include information he got from his counselees as they "confess the sin of another person" to him in his special role of "counselor."

In the following case, Tripp has figured out that Joe craves respect from others.

> Joe was the kind of guy who lived for the respect of other people. The way he sought to get it at home was by establishing a violent autocracy (though what he got was more fear than respect). Outside the home Joe was known as a real servant, a guy who would give you the shirt off his back. People at Joe and Sarah's church found it hard to believe that he could be capable of the things Sarah said he was doing with her and the children (*IRH*, 176-177).

Here is an example of a kangaroo court and judging another person's heart. Generally in such situations there is some truth and some exaggeration. Tripp does not give enough information to support his assumption that Joe craved respect, and, even if he had lots of information that may seem to lead in that direction, Tripp is still guessing. Only God knows! While sin comes from within, it is also stimulated by different environments. Joe may have received cooperation in the church environment and resistance at home. Nevertheless, in any situation such as this, one does not need to listen to unloving, sinful speaking about a spouse in order to help a couple move into the direction of a godly marriage.

Tripp uses the next case for "organizing data biblically" (*IRH*, 188-189). He says:

> Imagine that Greta, a woman from church, asks to talk to you. She is concerned about her husband John, who has an increasingly short fuse. He yells at her and the children at the drop of a hat. He is critical and demanding. He is spending more time at work, and most of his home time is spent on the computers. When she asks John

> what is wrong, he says that life stinks. Greta says that John's dad was a negative guy who thought that people were out to get him. John was not like that when she married him, but Greta is afraid he is turning into his father. When Greta asks John how she can help him, all he says is, "Just give me a little space so I can breathe" (*IRH*, 188).

There is no acknowledgment that Greta's complaining about her husband is dishonoring to her husband and to her father-in-law, or that this is a kangaroo court proceeding, or that this is biased gossip, even if there is some truth in what she said. However, this is a case ripe for digging and delving. Therefore, Tripp uses it to show how to organize data, as if he is dealing with factual information rather than a one-sided, distorted, exaggerated, and/or incendiary description. Interestingly in this illustration **the questions all have to do with the husband who is not there**. The question "What is going on?" is where Tripp puts "the information that describes the person's world (his circumstances), both past and present." Here is where he records information about John from what Greta has said about him, "raised by a negative, cynical father." Tripp's question draws Greta into dishonoring her husband and father-in-law (Eph. 5:33; 6:2-3) and plucking down her house" (Prov. 14:1).

The next question having to do with the person's response again has to do with the person that is being talked about behind his back rather than with the one who is seeking help. The question, "What does the person think about what is going on?" draws the answer: "All we know about John so far in this category is that his wife reports that he says, 'Life stinks.'" Now for the "motives": "This includes what you know about the person's desires, goals, treasures, motives, values, and idols." However, Tripp admits that so far he does not know what John "means by 'a little space' or why he wants it" (*IRH*, 189). Nevertheless, if the couple is enticed into this kind of counseling, John will have plenty of opportunities to provide more data, which will likely contain much sinful speaking about his wife, parents, children, and people at work. Tripp is the expert here. He is the evaluator and the judge. What a place for the temptation of pride to come in without anyone noticing.

In one of Tripp's possible scenarios, "Dan comes to you concerned that Jim is doing things that are unbecoming of a Christian." After Dan reveals personal information about Jim, we find that "Dan has also been hurt that Jim has violated his confidence when he has shared personal things" (*IRH,* p. 222). What is the difference between Dan sharing personal things about Jim and Jim having shared personal things about Dan to the counselor? The difference must be that a "counselor" is the recipient of the sharing of "personal things" about another person, rather than just any old person. Counseling truly opens the door to all kinds of confidences being violated, as well as gossip and other forms of sinful communication (Prov. 11:13; Eph. 4:29).

Regarding knowing another person biblically, the apostle Paul said, "Wherefore henceforth know we no man after the flesh: yea, though we have known Christ after the flesh, yet now henceforth know we him no more. Therefore if any man be in Christ, he is a new creature: old things are passed away; behold, all things are become new" (2 Cor. 5:16-17). Nevertheless, Tripp's "good questions" seek information about the flesh and therefore generally lead to evil sinful speaking about others. He is evidently hoping that, by knowing his counselees according to the flesh, he might be able to direct them to walk after the Spirit. However, so much attention given to the flesh increases its strength. This is why Tripp has counseled people over extended periods of time. He appears to be trying to give life to the new man by feeding and fixing the old.

Tripp declares:

> Asking good questions *is* doing the work of change. Through them, we give sight to blind eyes and understanding to dull minds, we soften hardened hearts, encourage flagging souls, and stir hunger that can only be filled by the truth. This not only builds a platform for the work the Messiah does through us—it *is* that work? (*IRH*, 173, italics his.)

In other words, Tripp is convinced that he is doing the Messiah's work through asking such questions. However, we do not see Jesus asking the kinds of questions that would elicit evil speaking about other people. Data gathering that depends on and elicits evil speaking about others feeds the flesh and comes from the world of psychotherapy, group therapy, media talk shows, and a wide range of so-called biblical counseling, such as promoted by Tripp and others. Nevertheless, Tripp is convinced that this kind of counseling is the Messiah's work and that a counselor is thus called to "incarnate Christ" (*IRH*, 97, 126, 128, 207, 269). Yet Christ would never encourage sinful speaking by His questioning.

Deceptive Dependence on Counselee's Self-Disclosure

Tripp insists that personal things, including private information about others (which may or may not be accurate), must be disclosed. He says: "We learn to ask questions that cannot be answered without self-disclosure" (*IRH* 273). He supposes that through the counselees' self-disclosure he will be able to know them better than they know themselves—as if he will know them inside and out. Although he will **not** know them better than they know themselves, simply knowing private information about other people puts Tripp in a power position. Furthermore, counselees will trust what he says because of his claim to be able to recognize aspects of their inner person. While Tripp becomes dependent on their self-disclosure, his counselees become dependent on him.

Tripp claims to "filter everything we learn about people through the grid of Scripture," because the goal is "not only to know others biblically, but to help them know themselves in the same way" (*IRH* 273). Can one individual truly know another individual biblically by supposing that he can know the contents of another person's heart? **This is utter self-deception. Moreover, this is God's territory! Humans can only guess, surmise, and draw subjective conclusions.**

Tripp majors is on diagnosing the heart by searching out the so-called idols of the heart, which can only rule the old man or the flesh. This ends up being a piecemeal project that may simply adjust the flesh into a more Christian-like appearance. The focus continues to be self-centered rather than Christ-centered. In this process individuals are trying to change themselves by gaining insight into their deceptive hearts through the help of another Christian, who is also plagued with a deceptive heart; instead of saying "I am crucified with Christ: nevertheless I live; yet not I, but Christ liveth in me: and the life which I now live in the flesh I live by the faith of the Son of God, who loved me, and gave himself for me" (Gal. 2:20).

Tripp says, "Until the idol is removed, it will distort and obscure everything else in the person's life" (*IRH,* 68). He identifies an "idol of the heart" as "*anything that rules me other than God*" (*IRH*, 66, italics his) and contends that "this idolatry is hidden. It is deceptive; it exists underground" (*IRH*, 67). However, one does not have to analyze the heart through hunting out a myriad of idols in order to walk according to the Spirit. These so-called idols (motivating, ruling desires, etc.) are only inner expressions of the flesh or "the old man." Jesus took care of the matter fully and the New Testament clearly tells believers all they need to know about walking according to the new life in Christ, without extensive analysis of possible idols lurking in the hidden depths, because they can only be lurking in the flesh, the old man, which is corrupt and must be put off (Eph. 4:22).

Tripp says, "Whenever counseling forgets the idols of the heart and focuses solely on horizontal human problems, needs, and difficulties, then counseling itself becomes part of the problem, not part of the solution. It will tend to strengthen and institutionalize that idolatry" ("Wisdom in Counseling," 8). In response we would say that, whenever counseling searches for the idols of the heart by spending lots of time talking about "horizontal human problems, needs, and difficulties" in order to supply the counselor with external clues to what idol might be at work, the counseling harms human relationships and strengthens the flesh.

Disdainful One-Upmanship.

Throughout his article "Wisdom in Counseling," Tripp refers to the counselee as the "fool" because "Sin reduces us to fools."[5] As one can see from the title of his article, wisdom flows from the counselor, who is the wise one in contrast to the foolish counselees. Not only does Tripp elevate his method of counseling and the importance of the counselor; he actually demeans counselees, who apparently cannot see themselves without a counselor revealing their hearts.

According to Tripp, in establishing the "ministry agenda," the counselor needs to know "what specific changes God is calling this person to make in this situation." He declares, "We cannot leave people to themselves or advise them from a distance" (*IRH*, 245). Tripp sounds as if these people would not be able to see or do anything without his guidance. Where is the Holy Spirit in this? And, how would Tripp know what God is calling another person to do unless it is extremely obvious. Even then, God may not have the obvious specific need for change high on His priority list. The Lord may purpose to change something else first. Because of his own deceptive heart, Tripp may glom onto the wrong so-called idol and help someone see something superficial, without recognizing that the person's heart is quite different from what Tripp sees, and that, if Tripp's agenda is followed, far less will probably be accomplished than by a fellow believer who has not learned Tripp's arm-of-the-flesh, sin-laden, insight-oriented methodology.

The idea that "we cannot leave people to themselves or advise them from a distance" is another one-upmanship of the counselor over the counselee. Tripp says, "We fail to recognize that, on their own, people often have a hard time applying biblical truths to their lives" (*IRH*, 245). Although people may "have a hard time" doing this, the Holy Spirit is in them to help them without Tripp's fleshly counseling methodology. In fact, the early church and true believers throughout the ages progressed in sanctification without the counseling rage that has recently overtaken the world and the church. Biblical ministry, free from the influence of psychological counseling theories and methodologies, no doubt did a better job. At least they did not depend on sinful speaking and inordinate introspection.

In describing what he has learned about a woman he calls Celia, Tripp takes a one-up position over Celia to the point of judging her through and through (*IRH*, 279-287). For example, Tripp says:

> Celia's life did not bear the fruit of repentance. First, she was not becoming a self-starter. She continued in sinful and destructive behaviors though we talked about them **on numerous occasions**. She would grudgingly admit wrong when confronted, but her confessions seldom resulted in new ways of responding. Second, Celia **remained defensive**. She continued to have a hard time receiving my biblical evaluation of her. She accused me of not understanding her, of not believing her, or of taking another's side. Third,

> Celia did not have a teachable spirit (*IRH*, 286, bold added).

Notice that this continued "on numerous occasions" and that she "remained defensive" through many counseling sessions and that she was still resistant to what he thought he could see that she could not. And, typical of the response of many counselors, if things do not go well, it is the counselee's fault.

One can see a drastic contrast between Tripp's high view of himself and his one-down view of his "lowly counselee." He says:

> I will ask questions they would never ask and probe in places they would not know to probe. My questioning will flow out of biblical perspectives on people and their problems. **Here I image the Messiah as I seek to end the groping in darkness**. I am … helping blind eyes to see, with biblical clarity and depth, the heart's thoughts and motives (*IRH*, 278, bold added).

Wow! This sounds like the Pharisee praising God for the contrast between himself as imaging the Messiah and the wretched counselee as one who is "groping in darkness."

What Tripp is describing throughout this section of the book is the corruption of Celia's flesh, which is similar to the corruption of all flesh, including his and ours. Because of the pervasive influence of insight therapy, Tripp believes he must expose Celia to herself so that she can change. But what he is attempting to expose is her flesh, which in essence neither he nor she can fully know and which simply needs to be put off rather than analyzed and dissected into idols.

Rather than weeks of counseling to expose her inner intentions and motives, one could help Celia see the difference between walking after the Spirit and walking according to the flesh. Rather than focusing on her corruption, the counselor could teach her about the new life in Christ. Teaching the truths of the new life would give opportunity to strengthen her in the new life without delving into the unseen realm of the flesh, which is accurately described in Scripture (e.g., Jer. 17:9; Gal. 5:19-21; 2 Tim. 3:1-7). Then, with the understanding that this is the struggle of every believer, Celia could be encouraged to desire to walk according to the Spirit and begin to seek the Lord herself. It would be better to help her see the contrast between the flesh and the Spirit through the powerful, living Word so that, when she is thinking or doing something, she herself can compare that with Scripture.

There is one question that would help believers: "Am I reflecting Christ in my attitude, thoughts, words, and actions?" Such a question asked throughout the day could help believers learn to recognize when they are reverting to the flesh and then to follow the wonderful plan laid out in Scripture by following 1 John 1:9 and Ephesians 4:22-24. In this way the Holy Spirit uses the Word of God with or without fellow believers coming alongside to encourage them in the faith. Like all of us, Celia is still learning to walk by faith, but to read the excoriating analysis Tripp has set up for her makes it sound as if she is a pharisaical unbeliever who resists at every turn. Indeed there are some who are truly not saved and who will resist the truth, and in such instances the Gospel needs to be preached and explained, not in reference to every jot and tittle of the flesh, but in the way the Gospel is presented in Scripture, with the understanding that, as people hear the Gospel, the Holy Spirit will be working. For some the ministry will be life unto life and to others it will be death unto death (2 Cor. 2:16).

Depart from Deception and Put on Christ

What believers need to do is put off the flesh, which is continually deceptive. Tripp may identify all kinds of these expressions of the flesh by listening to complaints about parents, spouses, and others; but in converting them to idols that can be managed, he will be enabling counselees to strengthen their flesh and even their own self-deception. As they begin to see what Tripp thinks he sees inside them, they may think they truly know themselves, but be even further from the truth than they were when they first became his counselees.

In the context of not being able to know God apart from the Spirit of God, the apostle Paul writes: "For what man knoweth the things of a man, save the spirit of man which is in him? even so the things of God knoweth no man, but the Spirit of God" (1 Cor 2:11). This verse clearly rules out the idea that an individual can know the inner man of another person, i.e., "the spirit of man which is in him." Nevertheless, Tripp's writings give the strong impression that believers who are indwelt by the Holy Spirit cannot know themselves without an expert such as Tripp to reveal their inner hearts to them. One also gets the impression that, if believers are to minister to each other, they must know Tripp's special methods of gaining insight by eliciting a great deal of sinful communication (thereby leading fellow believers into sin) so that the one believer can supposedly know what idols of the heart might be ruling another believer.

Tripp says," "The heart of every person is a fount of competing desires. We rarely do anything with one simple motive" (*IRH*, 79). **That is certainly one reason to believe God—that the heart is so deceitful that only He can know it.** We fool ourselves to think we can know another person's set of competing desires at a given moment, because, in addition to there being competing desires at any one moment, there are many more moments of many more competing desires. One could build a high tower, according to Tripp, with all the possible idols of desire, but desires may shift around so much that their Tripp-identified idols would not be static enough to stand.

God created our minds in such complex ways and sin adds confusion to the complexity to the degree that the question, "Who can know it?" is spoken with the understanding or the implication that **no one but God can truly know the human heart.**

> The heart is deceitful above all things, and desperately wicked: who can know it? I the LORD search the heart, I try the reins, even to give every man according to his ways, and according to the fruit of his doings (Jer.17:9-10).

Just prior to Jeremiah 17:9-10 the Lord declares that a person is cursed if he trusts in man: "Thus saith the LORD; Cursed be the man that trusteth in man, and maketh flesh his arm, and whose heart departeth from the LORD" (Jer. 17:5). But, "Blessed is the man that trusteth in the LORD, and whose hope the LORD is" (Jer. 17:7). The heart of every man is "deceitful above all things, and desperately wicked." Therefore, trusting in another person to direct the ways of your heart is a sinful way to go, because this is God's territory. The trust is misplaced and the deceived heart of another person will not be able to diagnose the deceitful heart of one who is seeking anything outside of God.

Counseling that seeks to delve into another person's heart is in competition with God. The person is turning in the wrong direction. To minister Christ's life to one another is one thing, but to look to another person to discern the contents of one's heart is trusting in man. The people who do this for a living, as Tripp has done (for money), may earnestly desire to lead people in the right direction, but **if they propose to diagnose and treat the heart, they need to recognize that this is the Holy Spirit's prerogative and to see that their problem-centered, sin-saturated, psychoanalytically-sounding counseling is psycho-spiritual syncretism**.

8

Pastor Randy Patten

Pastor Randy Patten was the Executive Director of the National Association of Nouthetic Counselors (NANC) for sixteen years, which is now the Association of Certified Biblical Counselors (ACBC). Patten previously "served as a senior pastor for twelve years, followed by twelve years as a pastor to pastors and consultant to churches." In addition he was "a trainer and counselor at Faith Biblical Counseling Ministries in Lafayette, IN, for over twenty-four years."[1]

Patten conducted a recorded counseling session, in which he counsels Trey and Deb, portrayed by two "ministry staff members," who are well acquainted with the kinds of problems and conversations that go on in counseling.[2] Even though they attempt a "realistic portrayal," the session is not reality. It is improvisational playacting **designed to present a perfect example of nouthetic counseling with a predictable set of problems, questions, and responses**. The participants all know the nouthetic counseling routine. Therefore, even though this is a contrived counseling session, it does reveal what really goes on in biblical counseling. Since the content and progress of the biblical counseling video is controlled by three individuals thoroughly familiar with what ideal nouthetic counseling should look like, **the sessions are nouthetic counseling presented at its very best**. However, we will demonstrate that nouthetic counseling presented at its best has become an accepted venue for sinful communication freely expressing the deceitful heart of Jeremiah 17:9. **To do this we will discuss the videos as if the counseling sessions are for real.**

Gathering Data

At the beginning of the video, Patten describes the main things he tries to accomplish in the first session: "gather data," "discern the problems," "gain involvement" (e.g., establish rapport so that they will talk about their problems and then be open to the counselor's advice), "give hope," teach, and assign homework. He also says that he used the Personal Data Inventory form, which asks counselees to list the main problem, what they have already done about it, what they expect from their counseling, how they view themselves, and what other information the counselor should know. With the PDI in hand, Patten begins the session and tells Trey and Deb that he "always starts out with Proverbs 18:13" ("He that answereth a matter before he heareth it, it is folly and shame unto him"). This verse sets the stage for Patten to ask questions and for Trey and Deb to tell all without holding anything back. **However, in order to honestly and accurately hear the matter, all parties involved should really be heard and that includes those not present, such as parents, in-laws, other family members, friends, coworkers, etc.**

Patten says that he needs to "understand completely what's going on in your life" before giving any advice so that he won't be "a fool in God's eyes" or give them "lousy advice." However, to "**understand completely**," Patten and all counselors would need to hear from all the people their counselees talk about behind their backs. He has not done this. Counselors do not check out the details of the stories they have been told. It is impractical and usually impossible to do so. Thus counseling is rife with kangaroo court proceedings. Counselors believe their counselees, even though research demonstrates that counselees lie to their counselors and will obviously distort the truth to their own advantage.

As mentioned earlier, one psychotherapist with a sense of humor once said, "Ten percent of the time clients lie to their therapists and the other 90 percent of the time they distort the truth to make themselves look good." And how often does a counselor seek to corroborate possible slanderous sinful statements made in counseling? The flesh is very proficient at ignoring, justifying, or adjusting the facts of one's own sinfulness. Therefore, the Bible advises getting the facts before believing tales: "He that is first in his own cause seemeth just; but his neighbor cometh and searcheth him" (Prov. 18:17). Patten and the other six biblical counselors could not have discussed this verse with their counselees in reference to what they say about others.

With the PDI in hand, already loaded with some amount of sinful expression, Patten proceeds to ask his prying, probing questions that precipitate sinful communication on the part of the counselees. He asks for a "brief life history" beginning from when they were "born and raised." Because most people who enter counseling know that they are supposed to talk about problems, the negative aspects will emerge. And, because no parents are perfect, such counseling draws counselees into violating Ephesians 6:2-3: "Honor they father and mother…." Trey dishonors his parents by talking about their personal relationship with each other, which included "a lot of fighting." Even though later in the conversation Deb expresses a real fondness for her parents and even hesitates to criticize them, she nevertheless dishonors them by saying, "It's probably not a great marriage." Here is the context of those words:

> My parents spent a lot of time focused on us, their children. I didn't really see them communicate with each other that much…. It's probably not a great marriage…. Sometimes my mom will say things about my dad, but they really don't spend a lot of time talking to each other.

Notice that Deb seemed to be grasping for something wrong and may have thought she should see something wrong in her parents' marriage to help the counselor analyze how that may have affected hers. Thus she is enticed into giving an unkind evaluation of her parents in this kangaroo court counseling session.

Pressing for More Issues and Details

The subject of Trey and Deb's fighting leads Patten to ask them for details about the conflict in their own marriage, how they fight, and how often. While men are usually reluctant to share in counseling, Trey seems to do most of the talking here, probably because the person playing the part of Trey knows the scenario so well and because he is not really talking personally about himself in the video, but rather about the husband he is portraying. Trey again talks about his parents' fighting and says that he and Deb do it nearly every day. When Patten asks, "Do you throw things?" Trey fails to protect his wife and tattles on her instead, by saying. "I don't, but Deb does." Trey thereby violates his biblical responsibility as husband to love Deb as Christ loves the church (Eph. 5:25-27).

As the questions and conversation continue, sinful speaking spews forth as Trey accuses Deb's family of being "a big problem in our marriage" and goes on to describe how close Deb is to her family and how she is constantly visiting them. He then plays the victim and complains, "I don't feel like I have the ability to be a leader in my own home. I feel like I am constantly living in the shadow of Deb's mom and dad and primarily her dad." Deb just sits there while Trey dishonors her parents.

Patten then asks Deb, "Are you surprised by what he said?"

Deb answers, "Well, his family lives so far away," and Trey adds that they only live about 3 hours away.

At this point many people would not see anything wrong with the way this counseling is going. They would assume that the counselor needs all of this information. However, as they are sharing their experiences with the counselor, Trey is sinning against Deb by exposing her sinful behavior to a third party. In addition to failing to love Deb as Christ loves the church, as he says hurtful things about her parents, he also dishonors and accuses them by insinuating that they are a major reason for their problems.

As Patten moves on to another issue, one can see that he is simply gathering as much data as possible. He asks Deb "What's another issue?" She says, "Finances." Patten then says, "Explain that to me." So again Trey and Deb complain about each other. This is open season for Trey not to love his wife as Christ loves the church or even as he loves himself, as he complains about how she spends money; and it is open season for Deb to express disrespect for her husband in front of a third party when she says he gets upset when she buys something. The Jeremiah 17:9 syndrome with their deceitful hearts is active as both speak sinfully about each other.

Patten then turns again to the PDI and reads what Deb wrote: "We fight a lot. It seems like we don't like each other that much anymore." He then asks for more details, what might be the contributing factors. Deb is very general in her answer: "I don't know. It seems to be all the stupid little things—big things, yes, but little things."

As Patten continues to ask for other issues, they bring up the following ones: when to begin a family, how they handle finances, conflicts regarding holidays and in-laws, all of which involve sinful communication, primarily dishonoring each other and their parents. Throughout, Trey and Deb unnecessarily and detrimentally describe a whole host of issues, all the while complaining about others and each other and violating Scriptures that speak of how we are to treat one another in our conversation (Eph. 4:29, 31; 5:33; 1 Cor. 13:4-7).

Prying into Private Matters

In response to Patten asking for another issue, Trey says, **"I don't know how much you want to get into this, but I'm very dissatisfied with our sex life." Right on cue Patten says, "Describe."** Patten's word "describe" is a command for more details. This reveals how deeply worldly this counseling is and the extent to which psychological problem-centered counseling has been emulated and embraced by the church. As much as prying for details is expected and practiced in biblical counseling, details about a couple's intimacy should not be shared with a third party in counseling. Nevertheless, problem-centered counseling depends on such details even in these intimate areas.

Trey tells Patten that their sex life is "nonexistent." When asked how long, Trey complains, "For a couple of years. I mean we're lucky if it's once a month. I think there was one point in the last couple of years we didn't have—we had sex once in three months. And that's very frustrating." Here Trey is playing the victim while exposing his wife.

When asked if she agreed, Deb responds, "Yeah." So Patten asks, "Is it because you're not interested in her or you're not interested in him or is one being unresponsive to the other?"

Trey responds, "I would say she is never interested in sex."

Deb counters, "It's hard to be emotionally intimate with somebody and that's what matters for sex for me. I mean it's no—I just don't flip a switch and it's on."

The marriage bed is holy and for Trey to expose his wife the way he does is sinful. This kind of talk would surely make a woman feel she has been betrayed. Notice that when Deb tries to bring in the idea of intimacy and how fighting harms the intimacy, she is not as rude and crude as Trey. As Trey and Deb expose each other in this area of intimacy, Patten treats it merely as data—information for future sessions.

Trey and Deb continue to blame the other and justify self. Of course Patten wants even more details. After about an hour of questions precipitating sinful communication, further expressions of Jeremiah 17:9, and some teaching, Patten says, "Based upon what you said today, I estimate that I will want to meet with you 9, maybe 11 or 13 times." Patten is not only giving Trey and Deb an indication of how much time and work it will take for him to fix their marriage; but it also gives Trey and Deb the typical biblical counseling "hope" in the counselor's commitment and expertise and in the counseling process to solve their problems. He asks them to keep a log of the topics they argue about during the week. This initial counseling session had the following evidence of the Jeremiah 17:9 syndrome: dishonoring parents, expressions of self-love, sinful speaking, mote and beam self-bias, a victim mentality, and disregard for the feelings and reputation of others. Consider how much more there will be in Patten's proposed "9, maybe 11 or 13" additional counseling sessions.

Confronting and Commanding

During the video of a later contrived session, the counseling includes a discussion of Trey's TV habits.

Trey had not followed through with his Bible reading homework. When Patten asks Trey to describe his evening activities, he notes how much time Trey had spent watching TV. The aggressiveness of the interrogation would shame a real counselee. Patten, in one of his several direct, one-up, authoritative stances, issues the command, "No Bible, no TV." Trey shamefacedly commits himself to follow Patten's order. Evidently this kind of treatment is not only permissible, but it is presented as an example of how counselors should treat their counselees in nouthetic counseling.

Patten throughout this counseling enactment usurps and undermines Trey's spiritual headship. Instead of building Trey's spiritual headship, Patten is tearing it down by demeaning him in the presence of his wife who is to "see that she reverence her husband" (Eph. 5:33). Here Patten treats Trey as a one-down inferior to whom he barks an order. His treatment of Trey is one of numerous reasons why men do not want to be in counseling.[3] One of many reasons why traditional men do not want to be in counseling is that they are treated in unmanly ways. Patten's "No Bible, no TV" is a perfect example of undermining the husband in front of his wife. This is reason enough why the real Treys of the world do not return for counseling. Moreover, **the sinful communication expected and promoted in problem-centered counseling is reason enough for no one to be involved.**

9

The End of Sin-Saturated Counseling

We discredit the biblical counseling movement throughout Chapter 2 through Chapter 8 because of its problem-centered counseling that leads to sinful conversations. We gave many examples from their recorded counseling sessions that expose the sin-filled conversations that pervade their counseling. These seven chapters clearly reveal that much of what counselees are expected and prompted to say reeks with the kinds of communication condemned in Scripture. We document the grievous fact that these seven leaders of the biblical counseling movement, in being problem-centered, conduct sinful conversations with their counselees. Moreover, we repeat: **the very Bible verses that biblical counselors avoid (see Appendix D) are the ones that expose their counseling conversations as sinful!**

In spite of these obvious serious flaws of sinful counseling communication throughout the biblical counseling movement, there appears to a lack of awareness as to the seriousness of such sinful conversations. Moreover, there seems to be an unspoken agreement that biblical counselors are not to be critical of sinful practices within the movement. The lack of internal criticism is a sure sign of how weak the biblical counseling movement truly is. We challenge those in the biblical counseling movement to openly criticize the unbiblical practices and teachings of these seven leaders of the movement, document those errors as we have, and provide their names and organizations they represent.

Because all the leaders of the biblical counseling movement appear to be "holding hands" when it comes to internal criticisms of their leaders and of the leading BCM organizations, we have accused them of being "in cahoots."[1] "In cahoots" means "in partnership; in league."[2] The definition of "in partnership" is "being a partner with or in association with,"[3] and "in league" is "working together, often secretly."[4] **Call it what you will regarding the problem-centered counseling with its elicited sinful communication, the silence is deafening**. We are not saying that it is always an overt conspiracy, but rather an often covert (silent) concurrence. Nowhere can we find evidence of those in the biblical counseling movement raising a raucous over any grossly unbiblical practice by naming names. Even those who agree with us do not raise their voices in opposition to a variety of unbiblical practices in the movement or publicly name those individuals and organizations that are guilty. So we conclude that they are **In Cahoots!**

Psychological and Biblical Counseling Conversations

As we said earlier, Dr. Jay Adams set the gold standard for the latter-day biblical counseling movement after having been trained and mentored by psychotherapist

Dr. O. Hobart Mowrer, who was an atheist. The following is a common definition for the practice of psychotherapy.

> Psychotherapy—also called "talk therapy" or just plain therapy—is a process whereby psychological problems are treated through communication and relationship factors between an individual and a trained mental health professional. Modern psychotherapy is time-limited, focused, and usually occurs once a week for 45-50 minutes per session.[5]

Note that the subject of psychotherapy is "psychological problems" and the solution is sought through "talk"! In psychotherapy the talk is generally **unrestricted in content**, even though the tone and volume of what is said in couple's counseling may need to be restricted to restrain emotional expressions of their conflicts during the counseling session. Therefore **the content of conversations in psychotherapy usually becomes sinful and does not meet biblical standards regarding the tongue** (James 3:2-8)**.** Because psychotherapy is problem centered, much sinful talk about others is generally part of the process.

Also, note that in the cases of all seven counselees the same situation exists as in psychotherapy. **Just as in psychotherapy, the talk in biblical counseling is generally unrestricted in content**, even though the tone and volume of what is said in couple's counseling may need to be restricted to restrain emotional expressions of their conflicts during the counseling session. And similarly, **the content of conversations in biblical counseling usually becomes sinful and does not meet biblical**

standards regarding the tongue. Like psychotherapy, the process of biblical counseling involves sinful talk about others as a resultant part of the process. Understanding this copycatting of what occurs in the process of psychotherapy should give one a clear reason why the biblical counseling by the seven leaders of the BCM described in this book and their followers should be avoided by all Bible-believing Christians. **That is because counseling that invites and allows counselees to speak sinfully about others cannot be done without violating Scripture.**

The Onerous Ones

Along with the newly minted nouthetic counseling (1970) came other biblical counseling practices that are imitations of psychotherapy, rather than exhibitions of the love of God in the fellowship of the saints ministering to one another. Along with the inherent sinful speaking in counseling are the following onerous ones, which do not show forth the work of the Holy Spirit in the lives of believers.

Onerous One-Way Relationship

Psychotherapy is "a process whereby psychological problems are treated through communication and relationship factors." In addition to the sinful communication, the counselor/counselee relationship is diametrically different from normal relationships where there is reciprocity. The counselor directs the conversation, but does not participate on an equal plane as in normal conversations between friends or acquaintances, where the focus of attention may be shared between one another. In normal conversation there is close to equal time given to and taken by both parties. The down side of the counseling relationship is that it is not a normal relationship with the normal way conversations are carried on in the real world.

Although "there are no reliable statistics" on what is called "self-disclosure," it is considered to be unprofessional for a counselor to disclose her own personal issues to a counselee whether the time is paid for or not.[6] Counselees are in counseling to talk about their own problems and not to listen to a counselor's problems.

Regardless of how dull and boring the counselee may be, the counselor has the responsibility to listen thoughtfully and often to hang on every word the counselee utters in an effort to obtain an accurate understanding of the problem and to respond appropriately. Normal friends will seem mundane after a therapeutic love-in that can occur in counseling. Olds and Schwartz aptly describe such skewed relationships:

> The special partnership that allows a therapist to earn a good living and a patient to focus on neglected aspects of his life and experience would be a disaster outside of the office. Used as a template for other intimate relationships, it is selfish and self-absorbed. Other than therapists, only an occasional very self-sacrificing parent or a spouse who aspires to martyrdom is likely to sign on for that long term. A problem with psychotherapy is that it can make all other relationships look like they fall short when it comes to sustained, attentive caring and leave the patient circling back to therapy as the only relationship that is good enough.[7]

This is one reason why some counselees continue in therapy for many years. **Psychotherapy becomes a primary personal relationship that focuses on me and my life, and biblical counseling can do the same thing.** For many, it is a substitute for a close friend. It is lop-sided and enhances self-centeredness with numerous possibilities for sinful communication. **If one replaces the word "therapist' with "biblical counselor" and "psychotherapy" with "biblical counseling" the application would be the same.**

Onerous One Up/One Down

Another serious aspect of the artificial one-way relationship is the onerous one-up/one-down relationship in both psychological and biblical counseling. The psychotherapist or counselor is considered the expert, the authority with special knowledge and wisdom. This is an artificial hierarchy of the expert over the needy one. The psychotherapist as seer is not supported by the research, as we have demonstrated elsewhere.[8] It has an authoritative power invested by society. In fact, the world has elevated the psychotherapist to the place of high priest, and grievously many in the church have elevated biblical counselors to a higher plane than pastors, teachers, and elders, unless they are biblical counselors as well.

This one-up/one-down counseling has been replicated by the biblical counseling movement. Examples of this wrong relationship can be seen throughout the previous chapters in this book as counselors take undo authority over their counselees. However, when the Lord calls a believer to minister counsel to another believer, there is to be meekness and humility, not a demonstration of expertise or a show of superiority. Paul says: "Brethren, if a man be overtaken in a fault, ye which are spiritual, restore such an one in the spirit of meekness; considering thyself, lest thou also be tempted" (Galatians 6:1). Yes, believers are called to minister to one another through the gifts of ministry and as fellow believers encouraging one another in the faith, but even those in leadership stand on an equal plain at the foot of the cross, because it is the Lord who truly accomplishes the restoration and sanctification of the believer.

Onerous One Hour, Once a Week

The definition of psychotherapy mentions that "psychotherapy is a time-limited, focused, and usually occurs once a week for 45-50 minutes per session." The seven biblical counselors function in such a way that we can say that "biblical counseling is a time-limited, focused, and usually occurs once a week for 45-50 minutes per session." The time-limited weekly meeting, whether done in a church or in a separated-from-the-church counseling center, is a further replication of psychotherapy and gives an unbiblical structured professional air to the meeting.

Why a fifty-minute hour? The fifty-minute hour is a device that meets the needs of the psychotherapist or biblical counselor to regulate the flow of clients for convenience and income when a fee is charged. The length of time benefits the counselor, not the client. The counseling relationship is governed by the clock, and the counselee or client who is late loses time from the already reduced hour. The time restraints of the system are primarily to the advantage of the therapist and some biblical counselors, who must see a number of clients or counselees throughout the day. Such restrictions do not lend themselves to developing caring relationships. The mark on the calendar and the hand on the clock must be followed, even if it means an interruption and "next please."

Here is another error that biblical counseling has inherited from its sibling psychotherapy. In a situation in which one Christian is ministering to another, time can be flexible. One does not turn on and off a relationship by the hand on the clock. Time is a precious gift by which we can demonstrate Christian love. Just giving time is a way of saying, "I care about you." And, the number of hours available through one or many members in a church supersedes what is available in psychotherapy or biblical counseling that runs by the clock.

Onerous One Right after Another

Worse than time-limited counseling sessions is the psychotherapy mimicking of one counselee after another being seen by a biblical counselor, which is even worse in a separated-from-the-church biblical counseling center. Since time and money are crucial to the professional psychotherapist, the regular process in a therapist's office is one person right after another. Clients know very well that they have been preceded by others and will be followed by more. Many biblical counselors operate on a similar schedule.

Counseling one right after another with large numbers of counselees always has and always will lead to superficial relationships lacking genuine compassion. It seems axiomatic that the greater the variety and numbers of counselees, the less effective one becomes. No amount of training will overcome the obstacle of numbers. Just as psychotherapy necessitates a one-right-after-another flow of individuals, the same can happen to biblical counselors who have a large counseling load. There is no biblical example for this; no, not even the example of Moses, who was judging, not counseling.

There is a real contrast between a listener who has a calendar of appointments with many persons per week and a body of believers who freely minister God's grace to one another without the necessity to see many people by appointment.

Onerous One Fixed Price

Another similarity between some in the biblical counseling movement and those in the psychological counseling movement is their charging a fee for the services. Charging fees or expecting donations for biblical counseling is totally unbiblical and indicates that a person's ministry has turned into a business to produce an income for the counselor at the expense and disadvantage of the person being counseled. We have written a number of articles revealing how sinful it is to charge for biblical counseling.[9]

This pay for service often ends up being pay for permission to sin with the tongue in the process of answering all the unnecessary delving, digging data gathering and prying, probing questions. Consider a fellow believer going to biblical counseling for help concerning a life issue? Can you imagine at the end a prayer, an Amen, and then a bill for services? Would Paul or the disciples have done such a thing? Absolutely not!

The content and controlling factor of any Christian ministry should be the Word of God:

> According as his divine power hath given unto us all things that pertain unto life and godliness, through the knowledge of him that hath called us to glory and virtue: Whereby are given unto us exceeding great and precious promises: that by these ye might be partakers of the divine nature, having escaped the corruption that is in the world through lust (2 Peter 1:3,4).

True biblical ministry involves the Word of God and the work of the Holy Spirit, sometimes directly to a person, but sometimes through another believer who knows Christ as Savior, ministered to one who receives it for deliverance and change. **True Christian ministry or the cure of souls is a sacred, spiritual work done by God, not man. It is a ministry to give; not to sell!**

Consider men and women whose lives are affected by fears, anxieties, depression, marital conflicts, family conflicts, or any one of a number of other traumas of life, some by virtue of their own sins and others by virtue of the sins of others, to be ministered the wisdom and grace of God and then to be told that they must pay for such ministry! **Can you imagine Jesus or His disciples praying for souls in such jeopardy and then saying, "Cash, check or credit card"? It boggles the imagination!**

Onerous One Culture-Bound Phenomenon

Problem-centered counseling and its penchant for sinful speaking is an American phenomenon. Eva Moskowitz reveals the contrast between "Americans' proclivity for the couch" and other contrasting nations world-wide. She says in her book *In Therapy We Trust: America's Obsession with Self-Fulfillment*:

> Though we recognize the therapeutic gospel's grip on our culture, we have little idea how we came to this point. Perhaps this is because the therapeutic has snuck up on us. Perhaps it is because we are only dimly aware that America has not always been obsessed with the psyche. But our therapeutic faith is neither timeless nor universal. Our nation has not always been so preoccupied with personal dilemmas and emotional cures, nor are other nations so preoccupied today. The citizens of Asia, Africa, and Europe do not share Americans' proclivity for the couch. There are fewer psychological professionals in China, Israel, and Korea combined, for example, than there are sex and art therapists in America.[10]

Although corrupt-talk counseling is an American activity, other countries are beginning to adopt it because of American influence. While it is on the increase, there has been little of this counseling in East Asian countries. One major reason it is almost non-existent there is because East Asians have typically **not** been **self-oriented**. They have typically been **we-oriented**, while Americans are typically **me-centered**. Also, the culture and tradition of East Asians has been to regard the family as sacred. Therefore one would not blame family or parents for one's present life problems.

One specialist writing on psychological counseling in Japan refers to the "family's sacrosanct character" and the reluctance to blame "a parent or parent's role in a patient's neurosis or, especially, the ways in which a maternal figure may not be all-loving and good." The article says, "A Japanese, instead of investigating his past, romanticizes it: Instead of analyzing his early childhood, he creates fictions about it." The contrast to American individualism is seen in the following: "Even for [Japanese] adults, expressions of individuality are often considered signs of selfish immaturity."[11]

Many Latin American cultures also represent a contrast to the American **"me" culture**. While there are some regional differences, Latin American cultures are generally **"we" cultures**. Mexican writer Octavio Paz describes this tendency:

> I am another when I am, my actions are more mine if they are also everyone's. So that I can exist I must be the other, I must leave myself to look for myself among the others, those who would not exist if I did not, those who give me my own existence. I am not, there is no I, **always it is we**.[12] (Bold added.)

Sadly, the "me"culture of our country has clearly invaded the church. Instead of acting like the Body of Christ, many members are focused on their own lives and problems and turn to counseling that focuses on me and my problems and inevitably becomes sin-saturated with all its complaints about other people and circumstances.

The church has simply followed the world and its psychological counseling with what is called "biblical counseling." **In fact, if the psychological counseling movement did not exist and had not preceded the biblical counseling movement, the biblical counsel-**

ing movement would not have falsely retrofitted their unbiblical psychological ideas into Proverbs 18:13 and other verses to justify such corrupt communication wherein they cause their counselees to sin against God and others and then teach others to counsel the same way.

This form of sinful communication would never exist and persist as it does among Christians absent the "godfather" practices of the psychological counseling movement. **There is candidly no precedence in Scripture for this kind of sinful counseling, which should herald the end of the sinful communication of biblical counseling and, therefore, the end of the biblical counseling movement.**

The End of Biblical Counseling

The clear evidence from the previous seven chapters is that biblical counseling elicits, engenders, and thereby encourages sinful speaking and other forms of corrupt communication, which calls for its demise. The Bible never set up a pattern of two people meeting together to solve problems through the kind of sinful talk that goes on in biblical counseling. Too many in the church have viewed problems according to the secular view that is predominant in psychological counseling, in which one must talk and talk sinfully about self and others to find solutions to personal and interpersonal problems of living.

We live in an affluent society, which may be undermining the church more expansively and deeply than direct persecution. Affluence begets selfishness, which is at the bottom of much of both psychological and biblical counseling with its sinful speaking. Believers need to move away from a me-centered Christianity to a Christ-centered Christianity where problems of living will be seen as opportunities for Christ to work His will in believers, rather than for problems to be solved through sinful thinking and speaking. Too many Christians seem to have lost their goal to be conformed to the image of Christ. Are believers unwilling to die to the self and live for Christ? Although some biblical counseling may have that as an end goal, there is too much sinning along the way to get there, as the evil speaking feeds and justifies the flesh, which is to be counted dead (Rom. 6:7-11). Believers become like Christ by looking at Him: "But we all, with open face beholding as in a glass the glory of the Lord, are changed into the same image from glory to glory, even as by the Spirit of the Lord" (2 Cor. 3:18); not through the sinful communication of counseling.

Instead of biblical counseling, believers need solid preaching and teaching about the cross, the new life in Christ, and how to live the Christian life by grace through faith. Every believer is created to be a vessel of the very presence of God—to be able to say:

> I am crucified with Christ: nevertheless I live; yet not I, but Christ liveth in me: and the life which I now live in the flesh I live by the faith of the Son of God, who loved me, and gave himself for me." (Gal. 2:20.)

The Christian life is not simply for a person to have a better life; it is to please and serve God. God is gracious and good. He supplies all our needs. He loves us more than we can realize. Yet He created us for His grand purposes, which are far more significant than the petty things that are prone to occupy our hearts and minds. Too often our view shrinks because it is clouded by focusing on problems instead of on Christ—trying to get rid of problems rather than using them for spiritual growth.

God has provided a powerful and fruitful way to look at and to deal with the difficult issues of life. For personal and interpersonal problems, which are the primary ones that biblical counseling tries to solve through evil speaking, Jesus died and rose again to give believers new life. Every situation in life presents a choice to walk according to the spirit or the flesh. Every trial has the possibility of bringing forth much good if an individual truly seeks God's will. 1 Peter 1:7-8 encourages believers enduring persecution and other difficulties:

> That the trial of your faith, being much more precious than of gold that perisheth, though it be tried with fire, might be found unto praise and honour and glory at the appearing of Jesus Christ: Whom having not seen, ye love; in whom, though now ye see him not, yet believing, ye rejoice with joy unspeakable and full of glory:

Peter compares fiery trials of faith to the process of purifying gold even though a believer's faith far surpasses the value of gold. Obviously God views such trials as being valuable for spiritual growth. However, if people try to solve their problems through corrupt communication, they are operating according to the flesh and the trial may be wasted as far a spiritual growth is concerned.

Paul even rejoiced in suffering, as he said:

> Therefore being justified by faith, we have peace with God through our Lord Jesus Christ:

> By whom also we have access by faith into this grace wherein we stand, and rejoice in hope of the glory of God. And not only so, but we glory in tribulations also: knowing that tribulation worketh patience; And patience, experience; and experience, hope: And hope maketh not ashamed; because the love of God is shed abroad in our hearts by the Holy Ghost which is given unto us. (Rom. 5:1-5.)

Not only are there eternal benefits; some of the benefits come in this present life: patience, experience, hope, and the "love of God is shed abroad in our hearts by the Holy Ghost." Through trials believers may experience God's love more fully and become more able to love others with His love, which comes through the indwelling Holy Spirit. What greater love than this! People may seek experience with God through various means, but a sure way to experience God is through trials—trusting Him and leaning on Him. Quite often experience comes after the trials, when believers realize the changes God has worked in them through the trial.

Consider how many portions of Scripture talk about living the Christian life. Here is where the emphasis must be—encouraging one another to walk by faith and praying for one another. For instance, Paul prayed for the Colossians this way:

> For this cause we also, since the day we heard it, do not cease to pray for you, and to desire that ye might be filled with the knowledge of his will in all wisdom and spiritual understanding; That ye might walk worthy of the Lord unto all pleasing, being fruitful in every good work, and increasing

> in the knowledge of God; Strengthened with all might, according to his glorious power, unto all patience and longsuffering with joyfulness. (Col. 1:9-11.)

Notice the words: "Strengthened with all might, according to his glorious power, unto all patience and longsuffering with joyfulness." Obviously walking according to God's will and provisions is not necessarily an easy way. After all, it is a narrow way involving dying to self and living by Christ's indwelling life. Also notice how joyfulness comes from the Lord strengthening a believer through trials.

Believers need to be well taught in the Word, through which they may learn the value of trials. Preaching and teaching are so very important. **Pastors have been given a high calling: preaching and teaching God's Word!** And their pastoral care should be reflective of the teaching and preaching of God's Word—not reflective of sin-soaked counseling! As a pastor teaches God's Word to God's flock, those in his congregation will be equipped to handle their own trials by grace through faith and also to minister mutual care and encouragement to one another.

Believers also need a **purposeful daily walk** wherein they are cognizant of God's presence and power for walking according to the spirit. The mind and heart need constant nourishment and reminders throughout the day. Believers are prepared for spiritual warfare when they are wearing their spiritual armor and regularly using the shield lf faith and the sword, which is the Word of God. Just as a soldier must be constantly prepared for a surprise attack, so must Christians be ready by grace through faith. This preparation comes from a daily walk—a moment by moment walk of faith and obedience, which starts with the Lord in the morning and continues throughout the day with times of Bible reading, prayer, worship, thanksgiving, and reflection. The ongoing stance needs to be "Trust in the LORD with all thine heart; and lean not unto thine own understanding. In all thy ways acknowledge him, and he shall direct thy paths" (Prov. 3:5-6). As believers trust God, look to Him for wisdom, and acknowledge His presence and Who He Is, God Himself will show them the way both through an ordinary day and through any trials, tribulations, and sufferings that may come along.

Mutual care in the Body of Christ is also essential. If the church operates according to New Testament principles, it will provide opportunities for believers to help one another in a variety of ways. **Consider the great resources already in place in a local church in which believers are walking with the Lord**:

Being available 24/7 is possible when the ministry is shared among believers, rather than one person having a "case load." Several different people may be involved in ministering to an individual in need.

Visiting a person at home, hospital, or work place may occur naturally as necessary because these are simply fellow believers experiencing problems of living. Neither a specified place nor restricted office hours interfere with mutual care.

Shared meals and coffee/tea/refreshment time can be considered opportunities for fellowship and sharing both as fellow believers and as friends, where the conversations can be edifying—encouraging one another in faith instead of the corrupt communication of counseling.

Providing food, money, and such practical assistance as child or elder care, help with household chores, etc. are included in the benevolence activities of local churches. The person who ministers personally may be the one to perform these additional acts of love or they can be shared with other members of the Body of Christ.

Daily prayer for one another and opportunities to pray together personally or on the phone.

Expressions of love and care in the local fellowship, including hospitality, ongoing encouragement, and sending cards for various occasions (from congratulations to condolences).

Godly relationships in which believers are equal at the cross of Christ rather than in an artificial one-up/one-down position.

Relationships can continue on and develop further after the initial problems. These can be like family relationships. After all, the church is a family of believers who have the same heavenly Father.

The above are merely examples of what would be operating biblically and practically in a Bible-based fellowship. **Biblically-based mutual soul care will put to shame those who offer their 50-minute relationships, filled with corrupt communication,** which pale in comparison to what happens in a truly biblical local church. These are all in addition to the vital worshipping and fellowshipping together.

There is also an important matter of church leadership responsibilities, which include biblical teaching, worship, and, if necessary, biblical discipline. Those who minister in the Body of Christ are to be under the authority and leadership of the local church, whether they are ordained as pastor, teacher, or elder. Within the context of the church there is both leadership and accountability. However, in separate counseling centers, church leadership is absent. Presumably anyone can open a so-called biblical counseling office and sell services to fellow believers in the same way professional psychotherapists open offices apart from the authority and leadership of a church. Then, when Christians buy counseling services from these outside agencies, they do so without the leadership, protection, and accountability of a body of believers organized to perform the work of the ministry according to Ephesians 4:11-16.

Conclusion

We have written a number of books that describe what can be done in the local church by those who are members of the local fellowship.[13] **The local church is the place for preaching, teaching, and pastoral care for the edification of all believers, under the authority of the foundation laid by Scripture and as given by Jesus Christ.** As believers mature in the faith, they are equipped for mutual care of one another. All truly biblical ministry builds up the Body of Christ through preaching, teaching, evangelizing, and caring for one another through mutual encouragement, instruction, admonition, confession, repentance, forgiveness, restoration, consolation, and comfort, as believers remind one another of all that Christ has accomplished for them. When the goal is to edify, there is no room for corrupt communication, evil speaking, gossip, blame, or expressions of bitterness, unbiblical anger, or malice within pastoral or mutual care in the Body of Christ, as they occur in the biblical counseling movement. All would be done to glorify God and nurture the spiritual growth of believers into the image of Christ, rather than glorifying the counselor and nurturing the flesh.

"The End of Biblical Counseling" will come when the church returns to its high calling of evangelizing, preaching, teaching, and living the doctrines of the cross and the new life in Christ; when believers are learning to walk according to the spirit rather than the flesh; and when mutual care in the Body of Christ thrives. We pray that those believers who have a heart for personal ministry, who desire to strengthen fellow believers in their faith as they are struggling with the difficulties and trials of life, will give heed to these serious faults that impede rather than inspire spiritual growth. We further pray that those Christians who are psychotherapists will realize that they are in even greater biblical jeopardy than the biblical counselors.

Appendix A

Old Testament *Counsel*

In the Old Testament there are just five English words (translated from a number of Hebrew words) that seem to relate to the currently used term *counseling*. They are *counsel*, *counselled*, *counsellor*, *counsellors*, and *counsels*.[1] The words translated as *counsellor* and *counsellors* are used in reference to the person giving the counsel. The other ones have to do with what is counseled.

There are at least two ways to examine these words: in their original meaning and in their context. The most frequently used word and its derivatives can be translated as "advise, counsel, purpose, devise, plan."[2] The repeated usage of the word *counsel* is for decision making or to accomplish a goal. For instance, when Absalom conspired to take the kingdom away from his father and sought counsel, Ahithophel proposed a plan to pursue David, smite him, and then bring those who had followed David back to Absalom. However, when Absalom consulted Hushai about the plan, Hushai said, "The counsel that Ahithophel hath given is not good at this time." Hushai then proposed another plan by which Absalom, instead, would be defeated (2 Samuel 17).

Counsel had to do with plans, guidance, and advice. Psalm 1:1 says, "Blessed is the man that walketh not in the counsel of the ungodly." That is, do not follow the advice, guidance, or plans of the ungodly. Psalm 2:2 gives another example of counsel: "The kings of the earth set themselves, and the rulers take counsel together, against the Lord, and against his anointed." Here a group is devising a plan in opposition to God.

If one compares the actual, contextual use of the word *counsel*, as well as the words *counsels* and *counselled*, one will see a great contrast between the biblical use of those words and the current biblical counselors who counsel people in their daily problems of living, habitual sins, emotional-behavioral problems, or any other such terms one might use. While there may be times when biblical counselors devise plans, propose a course of action, and give advice, the current practice of biblical counseling contains elements that go beyond the biblical use of the word *counsel*.

The most often misused example to establish biblical counseling is found in Exodus 18:13-26. The passage begins with a picture of Moses as he "sat to judge the people" and as "the people stood by Moses from the morning unto the evening." Moses' father-in-law, Jethro, asked Moses why that was happening and Moses answered:

> Because the people come unto me to inquire of God: When they have a matter, they come unto me; and I judge between one and another, and I do make them know the statutes of God, and his laws. (Exodus 18:15-16.)

In other words, Moses was judging according to the law of God. The word *counsel* is not even used to describe what Moses was doing. The word *counsel* is not used until Jethro is ready to give advice and present a plan to Moses, when Jethro said to Moses: "Hearken now unto my voice, I will give thee counsel." Jethro then presented a plan for Moses to teach the ordinances of God to the people and to:

> . . . provide out of all the people able men, such as fear God, men of truth, hating covetousness; and place such over them, to be rulers of thousands, and rulers of hundreds, rulers of fifties, and rulers of tens: And let them judge the people at all seasons: and it shall be, that every great matter they shall bring unto thee, but every small matter they shall judge: so shall it be easier for thyself, and they shall bear the burden with thee. (Exodus 18:21, 22.)

One commentary says the following about Moses:

> Having been employed to redeem Israel out of the house of bondage, herein he is a further type of Christ, that he is employed as a lawgiver and a judge among them. (1) He was to answer enquiries, and to explain the laws of God that were already given them, concerning the Sabbath, the manna, &c., beside the laws of nature, relating both to piety and equity, *v* 15. Moses made them *know the statutes of God and his laws, v.* 16. His business was, not to make laws, but to make known God's laws; his place was but that of a servant. (2) He was to decide controversies, judging between a man and his fellow, *v* 16. And,

> if the people were as quarrelsome one with another as they were with God, no doubt he had a great many causes brought before him.[3]

It must also be remembered that this incident preceded Mt. Sinai and the receiving of the Ten Commandments. Moses was judging the people. He was resolving controversies when disagreements occurred. He was not counseling problems of living like a contemporary biblical counselor, but was judging according to the "ordinances and laws." While judging according to the "ordinances and laws" may be included in biblical counseling, there is a great difference between what Moses was doing and what present-day biblical counselors generally do. Examples of some of the differences are given in Part Two, which describes what goes on in problem-centered biblical counseling.

In their eagerness to justify what they do, those who refer to themselves as "biblical counselors" turn judges into counselors who follow a pattern that more resembles psychological counseling than judging by God's laws and ordinances. Many years ago, in our own eagerness for counseling according to the Word of God, we used Jethro's counsel to Moses to encourage pastors to share the burden of personal counsel with members of the body. We continue to believe that the principle of sharing the burden applies, but we now conclude that the story of Jethro's advice to Moses is misapplied as a justification for the methodology of what is currently called "biblical counseling."

Counselors in the church also use Isaiah 9:6 to justify their practice of counseling.

> For unto us a child is born, unto us a son is given: and the government shall be upon his shoulder: and his name shall be called Wonderful, Counsellor, The mighty God, The everlasting Father, The Prince of Peace. (Isaiah 9:6.)

Isaiah 9:6 prophetically describes the coming Messiah, the Lord Jesus Christ. In this passage Jesus is called "Wonderful, Counsellor." The authorized King James Version separates the words *wonderful* from *counselor* with a comma, but Hebrew scholars say that the word *wonderful* is used to describe *counselor*. Therefore we looked into the meaning of both words. The word *wonderful* is the translation of the Hebrew word *pele'*. The *Theological Wordbook of the Old Testament* defines the Hebrew word *pele'* as "wonder" and says that it is: "Always in a context of God's acts or words, except for Lam 1:9. The root appears most frequently in the Psalms."[4] Thus it has to do with the wonder of the miraculous. It is beyond the common meaning of *wonderful* in English.

The word *counselor* (KJV) is from the Hebrew word *yâ'ats*, which means "advise, counsel, purpose, devise, plan," and is translated by a word from the Greek *boule* family (word group) in the Septuagint (the Greek translation of the Old Testament). Jesus as counselor is unique in that He is the very Word of God who "was made flesh, and dwelt among us" (John 1:14). He did not practice counseling as those who call themselves "biblical counselors" today. There were no ongoing sessions centered around individual people's problems. He knew the heart and spoke forth the Word of Truth. Today we receive His counsel through the written Word together with the Holy

Spirit. The involvement of the Holy Spirit in the Lord's counsel can be seen in Isaiah 11:1-2:

> And there shall come forth a rod out of the stem of Jesse, and a Branch shall grow out of his roots: And the spirit of the LORD shall rest upon him, the spirit of wisdom and understanding, the spirit of counsel and might, the spirit of knowledge and of the fear of the LORD.

Jesus is the Branch, and the word translated *counsel* comes from a derivative of the same Hebrew word as translated *counsellor* in Isaiah 9:6. The connection is clearly seen between the Wonderful Counselor and the "spirit of counsel." Therefore, this Hebrew word group cannot be used to justify the kind of counseling that goes on today. Nevertheless, we can be confident that God will continue to give counsel through His Word and His Holy Spirit. That is why solid Bible preaching, teaching, and evangelizing are so vital today and must be an integral part of ministering to individuals, couples, and families in need.

Appendix B

New Testament *Counsel*

In the New Testament, there are three words used in translation that seem to relate to the currently used terms in counseling. They are *counsel*, *counsellor*, and *counsels*. One of these words (*counsellor*) has to do with the person or persons giving the counsel. The remaining two have to do with what is counseled. Nevertheless, there is no example of biblical counseling as it is practiced in the church today. The English word *counsel* is used 19 times in the New Testament (KJV, Strong's *Concordance*[1]) and each comes from the Greek *boule* word group, which means purpose, will, decision, resolution, counsel, or advice. If one looks under the word *counsel* in a concordance and then reads this New Testament word in the context of the verses listed, it will hardly be necessary to look in the Greek dictionary to understand the meaning.

In many instances the word *counsel* is used to describe the actions of those who opposed Jesus and His disciples. For instance, Matthew 27:1 says, "When the morning was come, all the chief priests and elders of the people took counsel together against Jesus to put him to death." The word translated *counsel* in that and similar passages refers to the idea of consulting together.

In contrast to the wicked counsel engaged in by the enemies of Christ is the counsel of God, such as in Ephesians 1:11, which speaks of believers "being predestinated according to the purpose of him who worketh all things after the counsel of his own will." The same word is used in Acts 20:27, when Paul says, "For I have not shunned to declare unto you all the counsel of God." Indeed some biblical counselors will declare much counsel of God in the process of their counseling, and that is what should go on in ministries among believers. Yet, again, that is only part of what occurs in contemporary biblical counseling. The contemporary use of *counsel* in reference to biblical counseling relates only distantly and tangentially to the meanings of the words used in the New Testament.

The word *counsellor* is used three times in the New Testament. Two of the times are used to describe Joseph of Arimathaea and refer to his position as a member of the Jewish Sanhedrin. The other verse is Romans 11:34: "For who hath known the mind of the Lord? or who hath been his counsellor?" In other words, who would be so arrogant as to think he could advise God?

The only other word used is *counsels*, which is used only once, in 1 Corinthians 4:5: "Therefore judge nothing before the time, until the Lord come, who both will bring to light the hidden things of darkness, and will make manifest the counsels of the hearts: and then shall every man have praise of God." It is simply the plural of *boule*, which means purpose, will, decision, resolution, counsel, or advice. In this context *counsels* would refer to inner advising, planning, and directing within the heart of man.

Obviously the New Testament use of the words translated as *counsel*, *counsellor*, and *counsels* do have shades of meaning in the Greek. However, in no instance does the use of those words justify what is currently called "biblical counseling" in the twenty-first century. We are not saying that these are the only words and examples associated with counseling in the Old and New Testaments. What we are saying is that there is no counseling with its roles of counselor and counselee found in the Bible as presently conducted by those who call themselves biblical counselors. One cannot use the biblical meaning of the above words to defend the practice of contemporary biblical counseling. These terms have been usurped from secular use, retrofitted to Scripture, and then rationalized to be biblical.

One of the root meanings of the Greek words *sumboulos* and *bouleutes* translated *counsellor* or *counselor* is adviser. If contemporary counselors, such as those in the BCM, functioned as in the Bible, a person or couple would come seeking advice. The advice would be given and that would be the end of it. There would not be a need for continually discussing and convincing followed by a number of problem-centered sessions as with the BCM.

Christ-centered ministry focuses on building one's faith through truth (see Part Three) to encourage the troubled individual to grow spiritually, mature in the faith, and deal with his/her own problems as others do in relationship with the Lord. When one compares how Jesus and Paul ministered with the way those in the BCM counsel, there is a dramatic difference. While they may do some similar things as Jesus and Paul did, those in the BCM counsel more like secular counselors than like Jesus and Paul.

Appendix C

Counselor, Counselee, Counseling

Rather than emphasizing counseling, the Scriptures emphasize teaching. For instance, Paul wrote to Timothy: "And the things that thou hast heard of me among many witnesses, the same commit thou to faithful men, who shall be able to teach others also" (2 Tim. 2:2). The older women were to teach the younger women: "To be discreet, chaste, keepers at home, good, obedient to their own husbands, that the word of God be not blasphemed" (Titus 2:5).

Some biblical counselors claim that they are simply teachers or that they are simply discipling other believers. If that is the case, why do they call themselves "counselors" and why do they follow the format of worldly counseling? While we see instances of teaching in Scripture, such instances do not resemble the process of counseling as it is practiced today, with weekly problem-centered appointments.

The word translated *teachers* is *didaskalos*. If teaching is what they do, why not call it "biblical teaching" instead of "biblical counseling"? By picking up the word *counselor*, the rest of the baggage comes along. And, counseling is a big attraction. That's where the prestige is in Christendom today. Counselors are often held in higher regard than pastors, both inside and outside the church. The desire is for an expert in understanding human problems and how to deal with them. **The assumption is that the trained counselor has special knowledge. The unspoken implication is that the pastor does not, unless he is trained in counseling.**

The special knowledge people seem to be looking for has to do with the soul itself, rather than external behavior. Among the biblical counselors there are those who counsel behavioristically and those who counsel analytically as they attempt to identify the idols of the heart. There are those who look for the answers to people's problems in their past and in their "unconscious." Some have attempted to control the field through certificates, diplomas, degrees, and organizations. However, there is no universal model or method of biblical counseling. **Each counselor uses the Bible according to some combination of personal experience, secular theories, biblical doctrines, and "common sense," as is done in *CTHC*. The common thread among them all is their problem centeredness with its sinful speaking.**

While those who call themselves "biblical counselors" may be operating according to Scripture to some degree, they do so **not** within a position delineated in Scripture, because the New Testament does not present the position of the contemporary counselor. If they do minister biblically to another believer, they do so simply as fellow believers or within ordained ministries presented in Scripture. **The replacement for psychological**

counseling is not biblical counseling. It is ministering the Word of God to one another in love, patience, and forbearance. It involves believers being equipped through the gifts of ministry.

***Counselor*, *counselee*, and *counseling* are words that have been empowered and given status by a secular therapeutic society and adopted by the biblical counseling movement. These three terms are imbedded in the fabric of the secular society and provide a façade of culturally sanctioned assets to the biblical counseling movement. They give an air of "professionalism" to the practice of biblical counseling.**

Christians need to move away from using the designations "biblical counseling" and "biblical counselor." The words *counseling* and *counselor* have become powerful symbols and suffer the same shortcomings within the church as they do outside the church. Because the terms *counsel* (verb form), *counselor*, *counselee*, and *counseling* have such strong roots, meanings, and ties to psychotherapy with no biblical basis for their use in ministry, we suggest replacing them with the following:

> *Counsel*: minister, evangelize, teach, pastor, disciple, come alongside, advise, encourage, admonish, exhort;
>
> *Counselor*: minister, evangelist, teacher, pastor, fellow believer, helper, elder, brother, sister, the one who ministers;
>
> *Counselee*: fellow believer, brother, sister (or, if not a believer, a possible convert), person, individual;

> *Counseling*: ministering, pastoring, evangelizing, teaching, encouraging, exhorting, admonishing, advising.

Although some of these terms are not in Scripture, at least they are not contaminated by association with the psychological counseling movement and are in harmony with what Scripture teaches.

Appendix D

Violated Bible Verses

Because of the kinds of information counselors seek, the questions they ask, and expectation of transparency in counseling, the counselor-led conversations are filled with many violations of Scriptures, including those cited below. **Moreover, these verses are rarely, if ever, quoted by biblical counselors or used to restrain sinful speaking during counseling.** Instead, it appears that neither counselors nor counselees care about whether or not what is said during counseling violates Scripture. Christian psychotherapists, who are licensed and restricted by the state, are in even greater violation.

Use the following verses to evaluate any counseling, biblical or psychological, that claims to be biblical or Christian or claims to not violate Scripture and note the content of the counseling conversations. **Note both the absence and frequent violation of these verses, as well as many others. We quote only a few of the many Bible verses avoided and violated by biblical counselors and even more so by psychological counselors.** There are numerous other verses, but the following are sufficient to show that the seven counselors reviewed in this book are guilty of not using these Scriptures either to guide the counseling or to restrain sinful speaking, which they elicit during counseling.

Deceitful Heart

Jeremiah 17:9-10: "The heart is deceitful above all things, and desperately wicked: who can know it? I the LORD search the heart, I try the reins, even to give every man according to his ways, and according to the fruit of his doings."

Words

Psalm 19:14: "Let the words of my mouth, and the meditation of my heart, be acceptable in thy sight, O Lord, my strength and my redeemer."

Proverbs 15:1: "A soft answer turneth away wrath: but grievous words stir up anger."

Ecclesiastes 5:2-3: (in context of vows): "Be not rash with thy mouth, and let not thine heart be hasty to utter anything before God: for God is in heaven, and thou upon earth: therefore let thy words be few."

Matthew 12:36-37: "But I say unto you, that every idle word that men shall speak, they shall give account thereof in the day of judgment. For by thy words thou shalt be justified, and by thy words thou shalt be condemned.

Ephesians 4:29: "Let no corrupt communication proceed out of your mouth, but that which is good to the use of edifying, that it may minister grace unto the hearers."

Colossians 4:6: "Let your speech be alway with grace, seasoned with salt, that ye may know how ye ought to answer every man."

Titus 3:2: "To speak evil of no man, to be no brawlers, but gentle, shewing all meekness unto all men."

James 3:2b, 6, 8: "If any man offend not in word, the same is a perfect man, and able also to bridle the whole body.... And the tongue is a fire, a world of iniquity: so is the tongue among our members, that it defileth the whole body, and setteth on fire the course of nature; and it is set on fire of hell.... But the tongue can no man tame; it is an unruly evil, full of deadly poison."

1 John 1:8: "If we say that we have no sin, we deceive ourselves, and the truth is not in us."

Talebearing

Leviticus 19:16: "Thou shalt not go up and down as a talebearer among thy people: neither shalt thou stand against the blood of thy neighbour: I am the LORD."

Proverbs 11:13: "A talebearer revealeth secrets: but he that is of a faithful spirit concealeth the matter."

Proverbs 18:8: "The words of a talebearer are as wounds, and they go down into the innermost parts of the belly."

Proverbs 18:17: "He that is first in his own cause seemeth just; but his neighbour cometh and searcheth him."

Proverbs 20:19: "He that goeth about as a talebearer revealeth secrets: therefore meddle not with him that flattereth with his lips."

Proverbs 25:18: "A man that beareth false witness against his neighbour is a maul, and a sword, and a sharp arrow."

Proverbs 26:22: "The words of a talebearer are as wounds, and they go down into the innermost parts of the belly."

2 Corinthians 13:1: "In the mouth of two or three witnesses shall every word be established."

Anger

Psalm 37:8: "Cease from anger, and forsake wrath: fret not thyself in any wise to do evil."

Proverbs 14:17: "He that is soon angry dealeth foolishly: and a man of wicked devices is hated."

Proverbs 15:1: "A soft answer turneth away wrath: but grievous words stir up anger."

Proverbs 15:18: "A wrathful man stirreth up strife: but he that is slow to anger appeaseth strife" (Prov. 15:18).

Proverbs 16:32: "He that is slow to anger is better than the mighty; and he that ruleth his spirit than he that taketh a city."

Proverbs 19:11: "The discretion of a man deferreth his anger; and it is his glory to pass over a transgression."

Proverbs 21:19: It is better to dwell in the wilderness, than with a contentious and an angry woman.

Proverbs 22:24-25: "Make no friendship with an angry man; and with a furious man thou shalt not go: Lest thou learn his ways, and get a snare to thy soul."

Proverbs 25:23: "The north wind driveth away rain: so doth an angry countenance a backbiting tongue."

Proverbs 27:15: "A continual dropping in a very rainy day and a contentious woman are alike."

Proverbs 29:22: "An angry man stirreth up strife, and a furious man aboundeth in transgression."

Ecclesiates 7:9: "Be not hasty in thy spirit to be angry: for anger resteth in the bosom of fools."

2 Corinthians 12:20: "...debates, envyings, wraths, strifes, backbitings, whisperings, swellings, tumults."

Ephesians. 4:26: "Be ye angry, and sin not: let not the sun go down upon your wrath."

Colossians 3:8: "But now ye also put off all these; anger, wrath, malice, blasphemy, filthy communication out of your mouth."

Parents

Exodus 20:12: "Honour thy father and thy mother: that thy days may be long upon the land which the LORD thy God giveth thee."

Deuteronomy 5:16: "Honour thy father and thy mother, as the LORD thy God hath commanded thee; that thy days may be prolonged, and that it may go well with thee, in the land which the LORD thy God giveth thee."

Matthew 15:4: "For God commanded, saying, Honour thy father and mother: and, He that curseth father or mother, let him die the death."

Matthew 19:19: "Honour thy father and thy mother: and, Thou shalt love thy neighbour as thyself."

Mark 7:10: "For Moses said, Honour thy father and thy mother; and, Whoso curseth father or mother, let him die the death."

Mark 10:19: "Thou knowest the commandments, Do not commit adultery, Do not kill, Do not steal, Do not bear false witness, Defraud not, Honour thy father and mother."

Luke 18:20: "Thou knowest the commandments.... Honour thy father and thy mother."

Ephesians 6:2-3: "Honour thy father and mother; (which is the first commandment with promise;) That it may be well with thee, and thou mayest live long on the earth."

Husband & Wife Relationship

Proverbs. 12:4: "A virtuous woman is a crown to her husband: but she that maketh ashamed is as rottenness in his bones."

Proverbs 14:1: "Every wise woman buildeth her house: but the foolish plucketh it down with her hands."

Proverbs 21:9: "It is better to dwell in a corner of the housetop, than with a brawling woman in a wide house."

1 Corinthians 11:33: "But I would have you know, that the head of every man is Christ; and the head of the woman is the man; and the head of Christ is God."

Ephesians 5:22-24: "Wives, submit yourselves unto your own husbands, as unto the Lord. For the husband is the head of the wife, even as Christ is the head of the church: and he is the saviour of the body. Therefore as the church is subject unto Christ, so let the wives be to their own husbands in every thing."

Ephesians 5:25-27: "Husbands, love your wives, even as Christ also loved the church, and gave himself for it; That he might sanctify and cleanse it with the washing of water by the word, That he might present it to himself a glorious church, not having spot, or wrinkle, or any such thing; but that it should be holy and without blemish."

Ephesians 5:28-30: "So ought men to love their wives as their own bodies. He that loveth his wife loveth himself. For no man ever yet hated his own flesh; but nourisheth and cherisheth it, even as the Lord the church: For we are members of his body, of his flesh, and of his bones."

Ephesians 5:31-32: "For this cause shall a man leave his father and mother, and shall be joined unto his wife, and they two shall be one flesh. This is a great mystery: but I speak concerning Christ and the church."

Ephesians 5:33: "Nevertheless let every one of you in particular so love his wife even as himself; and the wife see that she reverence her husband."

1 Peter 3:5: "For after this manner in the old time the holy women also, who trusted in God, adorned themselves, being in subjection unto their own husbands."

1 Peter 3:6: "Even as Sara obeyed Abraham, calling him lord: whose daughters ye are, as long as ye do well, and are not afraid with any amazement."

1 Peter 3:7: "Likewise, ye husbands, dwell with them according to knowledge, giving honour unto the wife, as unto the weaker vessel, and as being heirs together of the grace of life; that your prayers be not hindered."

Self-Love

2 Timothy 3:1-5: "This know also, that in the last days perilous times shall come. For men shall be lovers of their own selves, covetous, boasters, proud, blasphemers, disobedient to parents, unthankful, unholy, without natural affection, trucebreakers, false accusers, incontinent, fierce, despisers of those that are good, traitors, heady, highminded, lovers of pleasures more than lovers of God. Having a form of godliness, but denying the power thereof: from such turn away."

End Notes

Chapter 1 Sin Saturated Counseling

1 Jay E. Adams, "About this book...," *PsychoHeresy: The Psychological Seduction of Christianity*. Santa Barbara, CA: EastGate Publishers, 1987, endorsements page.

2 Jay E. Adams. *Grist from Adams's Mill*. Phillipsburg, NJ: Presbyterian and Reformed Publishing Co., 1983, p. 69.

3 Martin & Deidre Bobgan. *How to Counsel from Scripture*. Chicago, IL: Moody Press, 1985.

4 Martin & Deidre Bobgan. *Against "Biblical Counseling": For the Bible*. Santa Barbara, CA: EastGate Publishers, 1994, available at amazon.com.

5 Heath Lambert. *The Biblical Counseling Movement After Adams*. Wheaton: Crossway, 2012, p. 148.

6 Bobgan, *Against "Biblical Counseling": For the Bible, op. cit.* p. 87.

7 Albert Barnes. *Notes On the Bible*. e-Sword,

8 Charles J. Sykes. *A Nation of Victims: The Decay of the American Culture*. New York: St. Martin's Press, 1992.

9 Jean M. Twenge and W. Keith Campbell. *The Narcissism Epidemic: Living in the Age of Entitlement*. New York: Free Press, 2009, 2010.

10 Eva S. Moskowitz. *In Therapy We Trust: America's Obsession with Self-Fulfillment*. Baltimore: The Johns Hopkins University Press, 2001, p. 83.

Chapter 2 Dr. Jay Adams

1 Institute for Nouthetic Studies, http://www.nouthetic.org/.

2 Jay E. Adams. *Competent to Counsel*. Grand Rapids, MI: Baker Book House, 1970, p. xv.

3 "Counseling," google.com.

4 Jay E. Adams, "What is Biblical Counseling?" www.gateway-biblical-counseling.net/definition.html.

5 Jay E. Adams. *The Christian Counselor's New Testament*. Grand Rapids, MI: Baker Book House, 1977, 1980.

6 W. E. Vine. *The Expanded Vine's Expository Dictionary of New Testament Words*, John R. Kohlenberger III, ed. Minneapolis: Bethany House, 1984; Walter Bauer. *A Greek-English Lexicon of the New Testament and Other Early Christian Literature*, translated and adapted by William F. Arndt and F. Wilbur Gingrich, Second Edition revised and augmented by F. Wilbur Gingrich and Frederick W. Danker. Chicago: The University of Chicago Press, 1957, 1979.

7 Jay E. Adams, "What is Biblical Counseling?" *op. cit.*

8 Jay E. Adams. *The Case of the "Hopeless" Marriage: A Nouthetic Counseling Case from Beginning to End.* Stanley, NC: Timeless Texts, 2006. Subsequent references appear in the text with page numbers.

9 Carl Sherman, "Man's Last Stand: What Does It Take to Get a Guy into Therapy?" *Psychology Today*, Vol. 37, No. 4, p. 71.

10 Louann Brizendine. *The Female Brain.* New York: Morgan Road Books, 2006, book jacket.

11 Allen E. Bergin and Sol L. Garfield, "Overview, Trends, and Future Issues," in *Handbook of Psychotherapy and Behavior Change*, Fourth Edition. New York: John Wiley & Sons, Inc., 1994, p. 825.

12 Martin and Deidre Bobgan. *Against "Biblical Counseling": For the Bible.* Santa Barbara, CA: EastGate Publishers, 1994, Chapter 4, pp. 73-92.

13 Jay E. Adams. *Competent to Counsel.* Grand Rapids, MI: Baker Book House, 1970, p. 93.

14 Jay E. Adams. *The Christian Counselor's Manual.* Grand Rapids, MI: Baker Book House, 1973, p. 187.

15 Martin and Deidre Bobgan. *Person to Person Ministry: Soul Care in the Body of Christ.* Santa Barbara, CA: EastGate Publishers, 2009, pp. 56-59.

16 James Dobson, "Husband Who Feels Suffocated Needs To Be Set Free," *Spartanburg Herald-Journal*, Aug. 26, 1998. Online at http://www.uexpress.com/focusonthefamily/index.html?uc_full_date+20011111.

17 "Relationships," http://www.troubledwith.com.

18 Martin and Deidre Bobgan. *James Dobson's Gospel of Self-Esteem & Psychology.* Santa Barbara, CA: EastGate Publishers, 1998.

Chapter 3 Dr. David Powlison

1 "David Powlison," https://www.ccef.org/about/people/david-powlison.

2 "AACC & CCEF", http://pamweb.org/aacc_nanc.html.

3 Martin and Deidre Bobgan, *Against "Biblical Counseling": For the Bible.* Santa Barbara, CA: EastGate Publishers, 1994, pp. 106-108.

4 Martin Bobgan, "Dr. Eric L. Johnson," http://www.psychoheresy-aware.org/eric_johnson.html.

5 Martin and Deidre Bobgan, *Person to Person Ministry: Soul Care in the Body of Christ.* Santa Barbara, CA: EastGate Publishers, 2009, Chapter 19, "Separated-from-the-Church Biblical Counseling Centers," p. 73, and Chapter 20, "Charging Fees or Expecting Donations: pp. 74-79.

6 "Fees," https://www.ccef.org/counseling/main-office.

7 Martin and Deidre Bobgan, *Person to Person Ministry, op. cit.*, p. 74.

8 Heath Lambert. *The Biblical Counseling Movement after Adams.* Wheaton, IL: Crossway, 2012, pp.44, 47.

9 *Ibid.*, p. 76.

10 *Pulse*, Vol. 6, No. 4, Fall 1988, p. 3.

11 Paul Vitz, "Christianity and Psychoanalysis (Parts One and Two): Jesus As The Anti-Oedipus." *Journal of Psychology and Theology*, Vol. 12, No. 1, 1984.

12 Vitz in *The Christian Vision: Man in Society.* Lynne Morris, ed. Hillsdale: The Hillsdale College Press, 1989, p. 80.

13 David Powlison, "Idols of the Heart and 'Vanity Fair.'" *The Journal of Biblical Counseling*, Vol. 13, No. 2, Winter 1995, pp. 35-50. Subsequent references appear in the text with page numbers.

14 David Powlison, "Crucial Issues in Contemporary Biblical Counseling." *Journal of Pastoral Practice*, Vol. 9, No. 3, 1988, p. 76.

15 *Ibid.*, p. 77.

16 James Strong. *The Exhaustive Concordance of the Bible*. New York: Abingdon Press, 1890, 1894, 1967, pp. 506-507 (word references 1494, 1497).

17 Martin and Deidre Bobgan, *PsychoHeresy: The Psychological Seduction of Christians,* Revised Edition. Santa Barbara, CA: EastGate Publishers, 2012, Chapter 7, "Psychotherapy Is Religion," pp. 129-149.

18 Thomas Szasz. *The Myth of Psychotherapy*. Garden City: Anchor/Doubleday, 1978, p. 28.

19 Raymond J. Corsini and Alan J. Auerbach, eds. *Concise Encyclopedia of Psychology*. New York: John Wiley & Sons, Inc., 1996, 1998, p. 306.

20 *Ibid.*, p. 307.

21 Matthew Poole. *A Commentary on the Holy Bible, Vol. II: Psalms-Malachi* (1840). Peabody, MA: Hendrickson Publishers, Inc., 2008 printing, p. 698.

22 Charles J. Sykes. *A Nation of Victims: The Decay of the American Character*. New York: St. Martin's Press, 1992, p. 34.

23 E. Brooks Holifield. *A History of Pastoral Care In America: From Salvation to Self-Realization*. Nashville: Abingdon Press, 1983, p. 23.

24 Tana Dineen. *Manufacturing Victims*. Montreal, Canada: Robert Davies Publishing, 1996.

Chapter 4 Dr. Heath Lambert

1 Dr. Heath Lambert, https://biblicalcounseling.com/about/staff/dr-heath-lambert/.

2 Heath Lambert. *The Biblical Counseling Movement After Adams*. Wheaton: Crossway, 2012, p. 148.

3 Stuart Scott and Heath Lambert, eds. *Counseling the Hard Cases*. Nashville, TN: B&H Publishing Group, 2012, p. 86. Subsequent references appear in the text with page numbers.

4 "Documented," www.vocabulary.com/dictionary/documented.

5 Deborah A. Sichel, Lee S. Cohen, Laura M. Robertson, et al., "Prophylactic Estrogen in Recurrent Postpartum Affective Disorder." *Biological Psychiatry* , Vol. 38, No. 12, 1995, pp. 814-818.

6 Thomas Insel, "Spotlight on Postpartum Depression," NIMH, October 28, 2010, www.nimh.nih.gov.

7 *Ibid.*

8 Barbara Schildkrout, MD. *Masquerading Symptoms: Uncovering Physical Illnesses that Present as Psychological Symptoms.* Hoboken, NJ: John Wiley & Sons, 2014.

9 Heath Lambert, "Can Jesus Heal Mental Illness?" Part 3, Biblical Counseling Coalition, May 16, 2014, http://biblical counselingcoalition.org.

10 Martin and Deidre Bobgan. *Counseling the Hard Cases: A Critical Review.* Santa Barbara, CA: EastGate Publishers, 2016, Chapter 3, pp. 47-68.

11 Elizabeth Loftus interviewed in Ryan Howes, "The Malleability of Memory," *Psychotherapy Networker*, Vol. 38, No. 6, p. 67.

12 The Institute for Biblical Counseling & Discipleship website: www.ibcd.org.

13 Martin and Deidre Bobgan, "The Institute for Biblical Counseling & Discipleship: A Critical Review," *Psychoheresy Awareness Letter*, Vol. 23, No. 6, www.pamweb.org.

14 Joseph J Plaud, quoted by Tia Ghose, "Bye, Bye, Playboy Bunnies: 5 Ways Porn Affects the Brain," *LiveScience* 10/13/2015, http://www.livescience.com/52469-how-porn-affects-brains.html.

15 Ligonier Ministries, "The State of Theology: Theological Awareness Benchmark Study," *Research Report*, 10/24/2014, p. 4.

16 Bobgan, *Counseling the Hard Cases: A Critical Review*, Chapter 5, "Cross Gender Counseling.," pp. 89-113.

17 . Heath Lambert, "'Sarah' and Postpartum Depression" in *Counseling the Hard Cases*, *op. cit.*, Chapter 4

18 "Postpartum depression," www.mayoclinic.org

19 Julie Revelant,"The depression moms don't talk about," Fox News, www.foxnews.com

20 "Breastfeeding pain linked to postpartum depression," Fox News, www.foxnews.com.

21 Heath Lambert with Joshua Harris. *Finally Free*. Grand Rapids, MI: Zondervan, 2013, p 12.

Chapter 5 Dr. John Street

1 John Street, https://www.gracechurch.org/(X(1)S(3xq2r2lvm1njt4i5a3ehqpn2))/leader/Street/John?AspxAutoDetectCookieSupport=1.

2 "Ministry Highlights: Biblical Counseling Programs @ The Master's College," Biblical Counseling & Discipleship Association Southern California (BCDA-SoCal) Training Conference, Fall 2011, http://bcdasocal.org.

3 Martin and Deidre Bobgan. *Person to Person Ministry*. Santa Barbara, CA: EastGate Publishers, 2009, Part Two; Martin and Deidre Bobgan. *Stop Counseling! Start Ministering!* Santa Barbara, CA: EastGate Publishers, 2011, Chapter 3.

4 http://bcdasocal.org.

5 http://www.masters.edu.

6 Biblical Counseling & Discipleship Association Southern California (BCDA-SoCal) Training Conference, Fall 2011, *op. cit.*

7 John Street, "Actual Counseling Session: Clinical Depression," Audio #17, and "Clinical Depression Counseling Case, Part 2," Audio #27, BCDASoCal Training Conference, Fall 2011, *op. cit.* The quoted dialog from the counseling session with Joe and Julie is primarily from audio #17.

8 Brent Atkinson, "Brain to Brain," *Psychotherapy Networker*, Vol. 26, No. 5, p. 10.

9 Pastor Bruce Groves email.

10 Martin and Deidre Bobgan. *Christ-Centered Ministry*. Santa Barbara, CA: EastGate Publishers, 2004, pp. 42-43.

11 Bobgan. *Stop Counseling! Start Ministering! op cit.*, pp. 160-162.

12 John Street, "Gathering Data/Discerning the Problems Biblically," Video Session Four, BCDASoCal Training Conference, *op. cit.*

13 Jay E. Adams. *Competent to Minister*. Grand Rapids, MI: Baker Book House, 1970, p. 274.

14 Bobgan. *Person to Person Ministry, op. cit.,* pp. 66-68.

15 Randy Patten, "Biblical Counseling Observations," Faith Biblical Counseling, Faith Baptist church, Lafayette, Indiana, Session One.

16 Bobgan. *Stop Counseling! Start Ministering! op cit.*, p. 77.

17 Bobgan, *Person to Person Ministry, op cit.; Bobgan, Stop Counseling! Start Ministering! op cit.*

18 Biblical Counseling & Discipleship Association Southern California (BCDA-SoCal) Training Conference, Fall 2011, http://bcdasocal.org.

19 John Street, "Actual Counseling Session: Clinical Depression," Audio #17, *op.cit.*

20 Sydney Walker 111. *A Dose of Sanity*. New York: John Wiley & Sons, Inc., 1996; Martin and Deidre Bobgan, "*Christ or Therapy*," Parts One and Two, *Psycho-Heresy Awareness Letter*, Vol. 19, Nos. 5 & 6, www.psychoheresy-aware.org.

21 "Idiopathic" in Wikipedia, www.en.wikipedia.org/wiki/Idiopathic.

22 Melinda Beck, "Confusing Medical Ailments with Mental Illness," *Wall Street Journal*, August 9, 2011, p. D-1.

23 *Ibid.*, pp. D-1, D-4.

24 Personal email.

25 John Street, "Gathering Data: Discerning Problems Biblically," Video Session Four, BCDASoCal Training Conference, *op. cit.*

26 Harvard Medical School *Mental Health Letter*, Vol. 2, No. 12, June, 1986, p. 1.

27 E. Fuller Torrey. *Surviving Schizophrenia*, 5th Edition. New York: Harper. 2006. p. 156.

28 E. Fuller Torrey email 9/13/12.

Chapter 6 Dr. Jim Newheiser

1 https://ibcd.org/presenter/jim.newheiser/.

2 The Institute for Biblical Counseling & Discipleship website: www.ibcd.org.

3 Martin and Deidre Bobgan. *Against "Biblical Counseling": For the Bible*. Santa Barbara, CA: EastGate Publishers, 1994; *Christ-Centered Ministry versus Problem-Centered Counseling*. Santa Barbara, CA: EastGate Publishers, 2004; *Person to Person Ministry: Soul Care in the Body of Christ*, Santa Barbara, CA: EastGate Publishers , 2009; *Stop Counseling! Start Ministering!* Santa Barbara, CA: EastGate Publishers, 2011; *PsychoHeresy Awareness Letter* articles, www.pamweb.org.

4 *Ibid.* When referring to what those in the Biblical Counseling Movement do, we use their terms of *counselor*, *counseling*, and *counselee*.

5 There is no such ministry office of Biblical *Counselor* in the New Testament.

6 David Powlison, "Cure of Souls (and the Modern Psychotherapies)," www.ccef.org/cure-souls-and-modern-psychotherapies.

7 Phone call to IBCD 7/17/2015.

8 Jim Newheiser. *Care & Discipleship Resource Handbook*, Escondido, CA: IBCD, 2014.

9 "Born Again Adults Less Likely to Co-Habit, Just as Likely to Divorce," Barna Research Online, August 6, 2001, www.barna.org.

10 Richard Simon, "From the Editor," *Psychotherapy Networker*, Vol. 26, No. 6, p. 2.

11 Brent Atkinson," "Brain to Brain," *Psychotherapy Networker*, Vol. 26, No. 5, p. 40.

12 Jim Newheiser. *Care & Discipleship Resource Handbook*, Escondido, CA: IBCD, 2014, p. 109..

13 Elizabeth Loftus. *Memory: Surprising New Insights into How We Remember and Why We Forget*. Reading, MA: Addison-Wesley Publishing Company, 1980.

14 Jay Efran and Rob Fauber, "Spitting in the Client's Soup," *Psychotherapy Networker*, Vol. 39, No. 2, p., 33.

15 Mary Sykes Wylie. "CBT Path out of Depression," *Psychotherapy Networker*, Vol. 38, No. 6, p., 39.

16 Martin and Deidre Bobgan. *Stop Counseling! Start Ministering!* Santa Barbara, CA: EastGate Publishers, 2011, Chapter Three; "A Critical Review of The Master's College & Seminary Biblical Counseling Program" *PsychoHeresy Awareness Letter*, Vol. 20, No. 4.

17 Stuart Scott and Heath Lambert, eds. *Counseling the Hard Cases*. Nashville, TN: B & H Publishing Group, 2012.

Chapter 7 Dr. Paul Tripp

1 Paul David Tripp, http://www.paultrippministries.org.

2 Paul David Tripp. *Instruments in the Redeemer's Hands*. Phillipsburg, NJ: P & R Publishing, 2002. Hereafter references will be indicated with *IRH* and page number in parentheses.

3 Paul David Tripp, "Identity and Story: A Counseling Transcript," *The Journal of Biblical Counseling*, Winter 2004, pp. 59ff. Hereafter references will be indicated with *IS* and page number in parentheses.

4 See Jeremiah 17:9 Syndrome in: Martin & Deidre Bobgan *Stop Counseling! Start Ministering!* Santa Barbara, CA: EastGate Publishers, 2011, pp. 53-63.

5 Paul Tripp, "Wisdom in Counseling," The Journal of Biblical Counseling, Vol. 19, No. 2, Winter 2001, p. 5.

Chapter 8 Pastor Randy Patten

1 "Randy Patten, http://biblicalcounselingcoalition.org/person/randy-patten/.

2 "Biblical Counseling Observations," Faith Biblical Counseling, Faith Baptist Church, Lafayette, Indiana, Session One.

Chapter 9 The End of Sin-Saturated Counseling

1 Martin and Deidre Bobgan. *Stop Counseling! Start Ministering!* Santa Barbara, CA: EastGate Publishers, 2011, p. 20.

2 *Webster's Encyclopedic Unabridged Dictionary of the English Language*. New York: Gramercy Books, 1996, p. 293.

3 *Ibid.*, p. 1415.

4 *Ibid.*, p. 1094.

5 Michael Herkov, "What is Psychotherapy?" PsychCentral, https://psychcentral.com/lib/what-is-psychotherapy/.

6 "Should Therapists Self-Disclose?" *Psychotherapy Networker*, Vol. 34, No. 2, p. 14.

7 Jacqueline Olds and Richard S. Schwartz. *The Lonely American*. Boston: Beacon Press, 2009, p. 166.

8 Martin and Deidre Bobgan. *PsychoHeresy: The Psychological Seduction of Christianity* (revised). Santa Barbara, CA: EastGate Publishers, 2012 (available at amazon.com).

9 Martin and Deidre Bobgan, "Pay for Prophecy?" www.psychohersy-aware.org/payproph72.html; "Biblical Counseling: Simoniacs and Pharisaics?" www.pamweb.org/bcsimony.html; "NANC & the APA," www.psychoheresy-aware.org/nancap65.html; "$$Simony & Biblical Counseling," www.pamweb.org/simonybc.html; "Charging for Biblical Counseling," www.pamweb.org/charge75/html; "Shut Down the 'Biblical Counseling' Movement?" www.pamweb.org/shutdown.html.

10 Eva S. Moskowitz. *In Therapy We Trust: America's Obsession with Self-Fulfillment*. Baltimore, MD: The John Hopkins University Press, 2001, p. 8.

11 Sudhir Kakar, "Western Science, Eastern Minds," *The Wilson Quarterly*, Vol. XV, No. 1, p. 114.

12 Skye Stephenson. *Understanding Spanish-Speaking South Americans: Bridging Hemispheres*. Yarmouth, ME: Intercultural Press, Inc., 2003, p. 47.

13 Martin and Deidre Bobgan. *Christ-Centered Ministry* (2003); *Competent to Minister: The Biblical Care of Souls* (1996); *Person to Person Ministry* (2009); *Stop Counseling! Start Ministering!* (2011). Santa Barbara, CA: EastGate Publishers.

Appendix A: Old Testament *Counsel*

1 All biblical references in this section are from the Authorized King James translation.

2 *The Words of the Old Testament*, Vol. 1. R. Laird Harris et al, eds. Chicago: Moody, 1980, p. 390.

3 *Matthew Henry's Commentary in One Volume*. Grand Rapids: Regency Reference Library, Zondervan Publishing House, 1960, p. 91.

4 R. Laird Harris, Gleason L. Archer, Jr., Bruce Waltke. *Theological Word Book of the Old Testament*. Chicago: Moody Press, 1980, Vol. 1, p. 723.

Appendix B: Old Testament *Counsel*

1 James Strong. *The Exhaustive Concordance*. New York: Abingdon Press, 1894, 1967.

www.ingramcontent.com/pod-product-compliance
Lightning Source LLC
Chambersburg PA
CBHW060206070426
42447CB00034B/2704

* 9 7 8 0 9 4 1 7 1 7 2 7 4 *